Furniture and Draperies in the Era of Jane Austen

Ackermann's Repository

OF

ARTS, LITERATURE, COMMERCE,

Manufactures, Fashions, and Politics

1809 - 1820

Designed and Edited by

Jody Gayle

📖 *Publications of the Past*

Publications of the Past, Inc.
Post Office Box 233
Columbia, MO 65205

For further information email
jody@jodygayle.com
or visit
www.JodyGayle.com

ISBN-13: 978-09884001-7-7
E-Book Edition: ISBN: 978-0-9884001-8-4
Cover: Grecian Furniture Plate from *Ackermann's Repository of Arts*, May 1816

Acknowledgements

My sincerest gratitude to the Philadelphia Museum of Art Library for permission to reintroduce the two-hundred-year-old *Ackermann's Repository of Arts* to a whole new group of readers.

A special thank you to the authors of Regency era fiction, who have continued to make the society, customs and fashions of early nineteenth century England vivid and vital to several generations of readers.

Contents

1809

1810

1811

1812

1812

1813

1813

1814

1815

1816

1816

1817

1818

1818

1819

1820

The rooms were lofty and handsome, and their furniture suitable to the fortune of their proprietor; but Elizabeth saw, with admiration of his taste, that it was neither gaudy nor uselessly fine; with less of splendour, and more real elegance, than the furniture of Rosings.

-- Jane Austen, *Pride and Prejudice*

Jane Austen cleverly used furniture and household furnishings in her novels to create humorous, intimate, uncomfortable and even sexually charged situations. In chapter after chapter, Austen utilized furniture to craft scenes and create drama by directing her characters around the room, to and from chairs, sofas, windows, fireplaces and even the pianoforte. Furniture was the stage dressing, sometimes even a character, for some of the most memorable moments in her novels. For instance, in the novel Persuasion, Mary Musgrove's sofa is one such essential piece. If not for Mary Musgrove's sofa, Anne Elliot and Captain Wentworth might never have rediscovered their love.

To learn about fashionable English furniture used in the early nineteenth century, one must dedicate some time to the highly popular publication *Ackermann's Repository of Arts*. The complete title, *Repository of Arts, Literature, Commerce, Manufactures, Fashions and Politics* was a monthly British periodical published from 1809-1828 by Rudolph Ackermann. This widely read publication contained articles devoted to the study of the arts, literature, commerce, manufacturing, politics and fashion. Each issue had of 60-80 pages, and included a significant amount of information provided by the readers, such as personal narratives, poems, opinion pieces and general interest articles.

The *Repository of Arts* frequently featured a section titled "Fashionable Furniture" that created an archive of superb hand-colored aquatint plates that depicted the latest fashions in furniture and draperies and included a description or general narrative on home design. In the 1809, *Ackermann's Repository* pointed out that "the sofa is an indispensible piece of furniture it not only ornaments, but becomes a comfort when tired and fatigued with study, writing, and reading – the exhausted mind can only be recruited by the occasional rest."

These illustrations were used as a guide to craftsmen and their clients in which the client could use the illustrations to order furniture, while selecting a particular fabric, color style and accessories. From 1809 to 1820, there were 144 issues of the *Repository of the Arts* published, and of those, just fewer than one hundred issues included furniture and drapery plates—every illustration is included in this book. Even after two hundred years after the era of Jane Austen we are still delighted and inspired by nineteenth century England. The illustrations in the *Repository of Arts* magazine were mainly for the haute ton, the very wealthy or newly-wealthy; however, they still drove what was considered fashionable at other levels of society. Jane Austen was certainly aware of the *Repository of Arts* magazine and perhaps used its pages to help develop her timeless stories.

The intent of this pictorial is to offer images exclusively from *Ackermann's Repository of Arts*. This book provides readers the opportunity to study the furniture and drapery plates from the era of Jane Austen, as well as read the original accompanying descriptions and narratives. It is important to note the descriptions are as they appeared in the magazine. The punctuation, spelling, sentence structure and even word usage sometimes varied from one issue to the next.

Considerable effort has been directed at precisely providing the text as it was originally written. The text is kept as it was published and the etchings have also not been altered.

Ackermann's Repository of Arts

The following article was first published in the first issue of the *Repository of Arts:* January 1809.

This plate is a representation of Mr. Ackermann's Shop, No. 101, Strand, and is the commencement of a series of plates intended to exhibit the principal shops of this great metropolis, in the same manner as the *Microcosm of London* represents the interior of the *public* buildings. It will afford the opportunity of entering into a partial detail of the different manufactures that are exposed in them for sale; and we flatter ourselves will form an useful, as well as interesting, part of our work. This shop stands upon part of the court-yard in front of which was Beaufort-House, formerly a town residence of the noble family whose name it bore, and was one of the great number of mansions which, at no very distant period, lined the bank of the Thames from Templebar to the city of Westminster. The noble and lofty apartments of the house, which commences at the back part of the shop, and a fine oak staircase of considerable dimensions, hear a testimony of its former magnificence. After it had ceased to be the residence of the Beaufort family, it was converted into the Fountain Tavern, a house of great celebrity in former days, and was remarkable from the circumstance of Lord Lovat stopping there to take in refreshment on his way from Westminster-Hall to the Tower, and writing with his diamond ring the following couplet upon a pane of glass in the great room:

> Oh! through what various scenes of life we run,
> Are wicked to great and being great undone!
> Simon Fraser

This room, which is 65 feet in length, 30 in width, and 24 in height, was formerly occupied by Mr. Shipley, brother to the bishop of that name; he kept a most respectable drawing academy here: among his pupils were, Mr. W Parr, who died at Rome, C. Smart, Esq. and the celebrated R. Cosway, Esq. R.A.: the latter had in his possession the pane of glass before-mentioned. A curious, but well-authenticated anecdote is related of Henry Parr's wife (H. Parr succeeded Shipley in this academy) who had been confined to the house upwards of nine years by a paralytic affection, which during that period entirely deprived her of speech. One day, in the absence of her husband, the servant-maid abruptly entering her apartment, told her that the adjoining house was on fire, which had such an effect upon her system, that her powers of utterance returned instantaneously, and she continued to enjoy them again to the day of her death, which did not happen for some year afterwards.

This room is famous on another account, having been the scene of Mr. Thelwall's early political lectures. When the interposition of government put a stop to this exhibition, Mr. A. purchased the lease, and it became once more the peaceful academy of drawing, upon a very extended scale, employing three masters in the separate branches of this art, one for figures, a second for landscape, and a third for architecture. But the increase of Mr. Ackermann's business as a publisher, printseller, and manufacturer of fancy articles, rendered the convenience of this room a warehouse a more desirable object than the profit to be derived from it as an academy. For eight or ten years previous to entering so largely in the fancy business, Mr. A. had been employed in furnishing the principal coachmakers with designs and models for new and improved carriages. Among many instances of his taste and abilities in this line, the state coach built for the Lord Lieutenant of Ireland, in 1790, which cost near 7000/. and one for the Lord Mayor of Dublin in the following year, were designed and modelled by him. It has been said, that Philip Godsal, Esq. who has the model of the Lord Lieutenant's coach, has actually refused one hundred guineas for it, and it is more than probable, he would not sell it for twice that sum.

During the period when the French emigrants were so numerous in this country, Mr. A. was among the first to strike out a liberal and easy mode of employing them, and he had seldom less than fifty noble, priests, and ladies of distinction, at work upon screens, card-racks, flower-stands, and other ornamental fancy-works of a similar nature. Since the decree permitting the return of the emigrants to France, this manufacture has been continued by native artists, who execute the work in a very superior style: but it is impossible in this place to notice the great variety of articles which it embraces. The public are referred to a catalogue of near 100 pages, which conveys every information that can be necessary, and will be our apology for omitting any further observations; we shall therefore only add, that since Mr. A. has given up the academy, he has substituted a portfolio of prints and drawings for the use of pupils and dilitanti, upon the plan of a circulating library of books, the terms of which areas follow: Yearly subscription.

4 Guineas,

Half-yearly ditto.. 2 ditto.

Quarterly ditto... l ditto.

The money paid at the time of subscribing. The subscribers are allowed to take the value of their subscription money in prints or drawings, and may change them as often as they please.

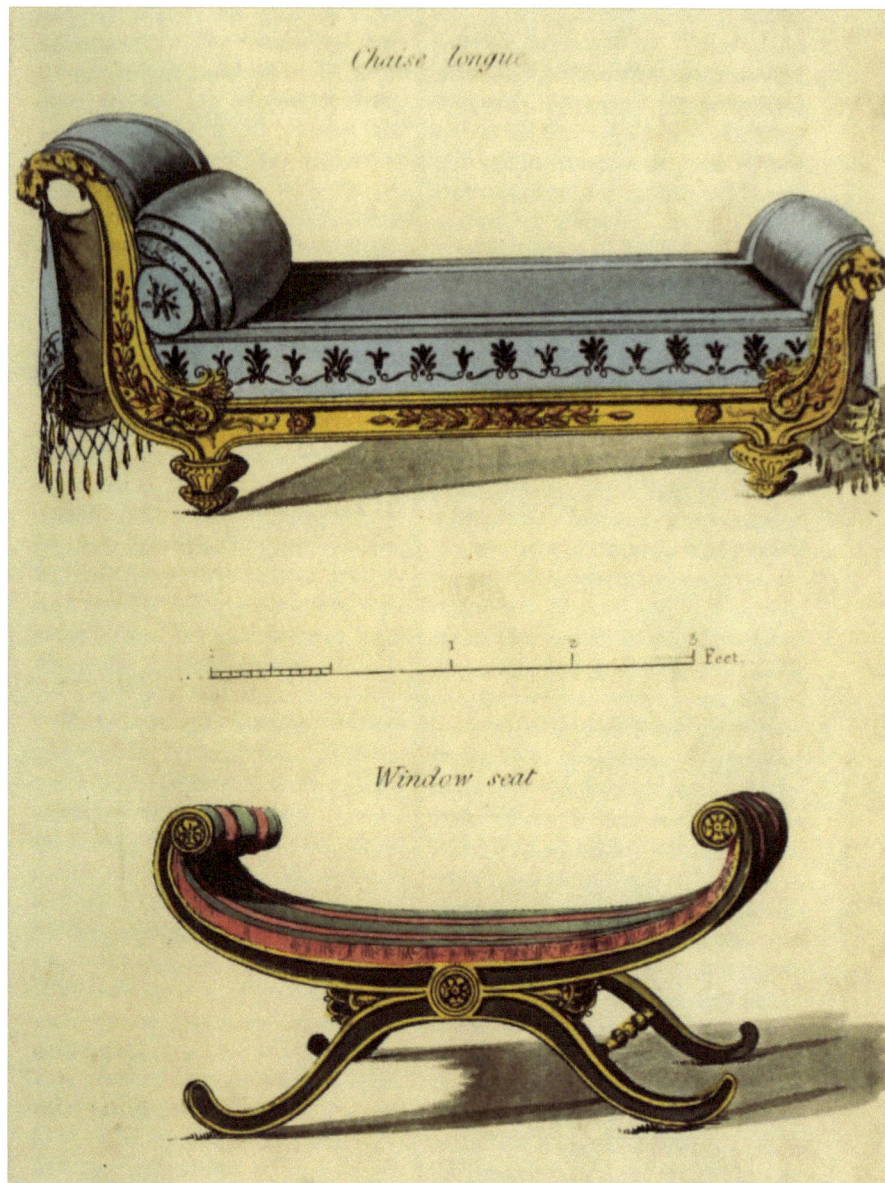

Chaise Longue
January 1809

CHAISE LONGUE

The design of the chaise longue is Grecian, and should be executed as to its frame- work wholly in mat and burnished gold, when chasteness of execution is desired; the ornaments may be finished in bronze metal, when a similar style has been adopted in the other furniture of the apartment. The covering here shewn is supposed to be of azure blue velvet, the ornaments being worked up in gold colour and bronze.

Each end has a Grecian mantle, to correspond with the covering, fringed with a gold-colour silk fringe. One side of this design being geometrical, a scale is added, from which every dimension may be obtained, observing that 28 inch. is its intended width.

WINDOW-SEAT

This design would have a very good effect executed in bronze, with the rosettes, fillets, and other ornament of the frame, in mat gold. It might be covered with green velvet, with stripes of rose colour. The design of this window-seat was furnished by Messrs. Morgan and Saunders, Catherine-street, Strand.

1

Fashion is ever creating change and variety in furniture. We observe with pleasure a more tasteful arrangement daily taking place; the gaudy colours of the chintz and calico furniture have given place to a more chaste style, in which two colours only are employed to produce the appearance of damask. The same style is adopting in carpets, giving apartments an uniform and pleasing appearance. Bronze still prevails as a ground-work for chairs, sofas, cabinets, &c and will always be classic when delicately and sparing assisted with gold ornaments. A great deal of black has been used in chairs, &c. but the appearance is harsh, and the contrast too violent to be approved by genuine and correct taste; its cheapness can alone make its use tolerable. Manchester coloured velvets, used for furniture and curtains, produce a rich effect. Poles richly decorated form the best and most fashionable supporters for draperies, and in all probability will continue throughout the present year. Other improvements will be noticed in our succeeding numbers.

In fitting up dining-rooms it has been suggested, that a new system is about to be adopted, in which the architecture and the furniture are rendered subservient to domestic comfort, as well as elegant arrangement. In the Morning Post, a few days since, is noticed a design now executing for the eating-room of a noble duke: it comprehends a space of sixty feet in length, from which twenty feet are taken by a colonnade of ten feet at each end. Ten feet forms the breast of the chimney; the remaining spaces on each side become recesses, three feet and a half deep, in which are placed architectural pedestals, supporting imitative granite columns. These pedestals are so contrived as to contain every necessary requisite, usually placed in what are called sarcophagus cellarets, with other conveniences, rendering the ingress and egress of domestics less troubles than is customary . The remaining spaces are appropriated to the side-boards: they are supported eight beautiful and strictly classic Grecian female Caryatides, under a frieze embellished by a Greek ornament of the present taste, executed in bronze metal. The vacuum underneath each side-board is corrected by the placing of elegant sarcophaguses adapted to the purpose of heating plates, &c. by contrivances from the flue of the chimney. The whole of these embellishments are intended to be executed in the most beautiful mahogany, relieved by ormolu inlay of ornaments and lines. Over each sideboard will be placed glasses of the most superb dimensions, in frames of bronze and gold; in the recesses and center of each glass are to be suspended cut-glass Grecian lamps of an unique design and execution. The carpet for the room is making at Axminster, from a design given by the architect.

LADIES SECRETAIRE.

PARLOR CHAIR.

Ladies' Secretaire
March 1809

LADIES' SECRETAIRE

This elegant appendage to the drawing-room or boudoir, should be made of rosewood, rich and varied in its grain. The female figures supporting the secretaire, and the lyres on the upper part, may be carved in wood, and finished in burnish and matt gold, to imitate or moulu. The ornaments on the drawers may be of metal, water gilt. The bottom part, has a mirror on the back, placed on a shelf, carved in the front, and ornamented with or moulu mouldings, supported on vase feet. The front of the secretaire drawer is decorated with or moulu handles, formed as wreaths of foliage; a star in the center, concealing the key-hole of the lock.

PARLOUR CHAIRS

This pattern, of Grecian form, is supposed to be of mahogany; the ornaments and the frame are made out in an inlay of ebony. The continued line from the top of the back, to the gilt ornaments on the front feet, should be paneled out be-twixt two beads. The ornament in center of the back may in part be carved, and the rest in ebony. The seat and back of the chair are stuffed and covered with red morocco leather, on which are printed Grecian ornaments in black.

GENERAL OBSERVATIONS

A considerable alteration has taken place in the style of fitting up apartments within these few months. Instead of a gaudy display in colouring, a more pleasing and chaste effect is produced in the union of two tints. This has been happily managed in calicoes, producing an appearance equal to silk, particularly in the richer and more brilliant colours. We have witnessed this effect in a full crimson damask pattern, lined with a blue embossed calico, the manufacture of Messrs. Dudding and Nelson. A similar taste has been followed with some success in paper-hanging, exhibiting a rich appearance, when finished with gold, or black and gold mouldings. Carpets, especially for principal apartments, have partially fallen into the same good taste.

This mode of furnishing, producing in the predominant features a composed and uniform effect, aids greatly the meubles of grand rooms, especially where gilding is introduced. Should silk become objectionable from its expence, we strongly recommend the use of these new patterns. They need only be seen to become approved, and are particularly calculated for candle-light effect.

DINING PARLOUR

In this apartment morone continues still in use, and the more so where economy is requisite; which article also has experienced an improvement by being embossed in a variety of patterns. This process, however, renders it less appropriate for drapery, unless there should be sufficient extent to form it with boldness. The coverings for floors are of crimson drugget, milled to a proper substance, and paneled with a border of black furniture cloth; producing a warm and rich appearance. The same arrangement is to been seen in the drawing-rooms of many of the haut ton, in various colours. Chandeliers of cut glass, on a metal framework, with ornaments of or moulu and bronze, are generally used for illuminating rooms, affording a brilliant and diffused light from the center of the ceiling.

For the preceding observations, we acknowledge ourselves indebted to Mr. G. Smith, whose classic taste in this line is evinced in his splendid work on furniture and decoration.

Window-Curtain
April 1809

WINDOW-CURTAIN

Is a representation of a window- curtain, the design of Mr. Allen of Pall-Mail, who has lately submitted to the public some of the most chaste and elegant patterns of calicoes we have ever seen. The taste displayed by him, in the manner of forming the drapery, his connection of the most vivid with the serenest colours, and the tout-ensemble of the production, are equally admirable. We are happy to see the classic elegance of the ancients revived amongst us.

This curtain is intended as an appropriation to a boudoir. It is composed of a ruby-coloured calico enriched with star-like figure of various black hues. It is lined with a newly invented print of an azure colour, strictly resembling a figured silk. The drapery has a Persian silk fringe of the colour of gold, united to a small portion of sable. The pole is suspended by silken cords attached to fashionable metal pins. It is scarcely necessary to mention, that if the apartment to be thus decorated has several windows, the intervals of the curtains must be filled up by a continuation of the blue silk mantle.

Art would suffer much in public esteem it unconnected with a proper display of their perfections. — Curtains, though originally invented for use only, because, with the improvements of literature, emblems of representations of military tents and religious veils. The former is partly intended in the present instance. The implements of instance judiciously placed, and shew that the interior is the residence of a chieftain. It is impossible, however, that a print should do perfect justice to the elegant repose of drapery; Vandyck, so celebrated in that line, fell short of a perfect imitation.

GENERAL OBSERVATIONS

In no department of furnishing has the inventive power of fancy been more assiduously employed, than in the disposition of draperies for windows, beds, alcoves, and other suitable objects. It is the elegance and the lightness of drapery that have given reputation to the most famous sculptors; and indeed their works are all but humble imitations of nature, who seems, even on a vast scale, to dispose her beauties with an ease almost approaching to negligence. It is on considerations that the heavy and cumbrous objects of furniture are giving place to airy and light designs. The large cornice, the ponderous mantle-piece, and massy chairs, yield the palm to modern inventions founded on the firm basis of observation of nature. – Those who study this unerring model, will find their reputation increased in proportion as they advance.

Sofa or French Bed
May 1809

SOFA OR FRENCH BED

The frame of this piece of furniture is of mahogany, the ornaments executed in metal gilt; the cushion bolsters, and ends, are covered with white satin; the outsides of the ends in blue, to suit the drapery suspended over the couch, having ornaments in gold-coloured velvet placed on them: a gold-coloured silk fringe is fixed on the scrolls. Over the couch is suspended a canopy, composed of ornamental gold moldings, a Vitrurian scroll occupying the frieze. The whole of these are carved in wood, and gilt, after the manner of or moulu, the ground being of blue velvet. A dome, composed of bold quilling, and covered with blue satin, surmounted with a coronet, carved and gilt, terminates the whole.

The furniture is of blue satin, lined with white lute-string, and should be trimmed with a narrow gold edging. A deep valance, after the Grecian taste, or blue velvet, bordered with gold-coloured velvet and ornaments, with a French fringe and tassels, completes this costly article, which should always be placed on a platform, covered with carpet the same as the room. A pedestal, painted as marble, is placed on one side, and ornamented with or moulu, serving as a table. The dome of the bed has a strong iron plate attached to it, with hooks which slip into sockets fixed in the wall, whereby it may be put up and taken down at pleasure, leaving only the sofa.

6

GENERAL OBSERVATIONS - May 1809

The taste for single colours, in silks or calicoes, still continues to prevail. Black chairs, ornamented with metal gilt, in various elegant devices, are in universal use, and certainly have a good effect, from their neatness; and there is hardly any apartment in which they may not be suitably placed.

Bronze and gold still continue in use in the more ornamental and decorative articles of tables, candelabras, glasses, and cornices for windows; and we still witness a taste for using draperies in continuation. Holding the antique as a ground-work for taste, a much lighter style evinces itself in modern works of art than has prevailed to some time; for which we are greatly indebted to Grecian school, and which in the space of a very few years, bids fair to give this country the pre-eminence, not only in execution, but also in design.

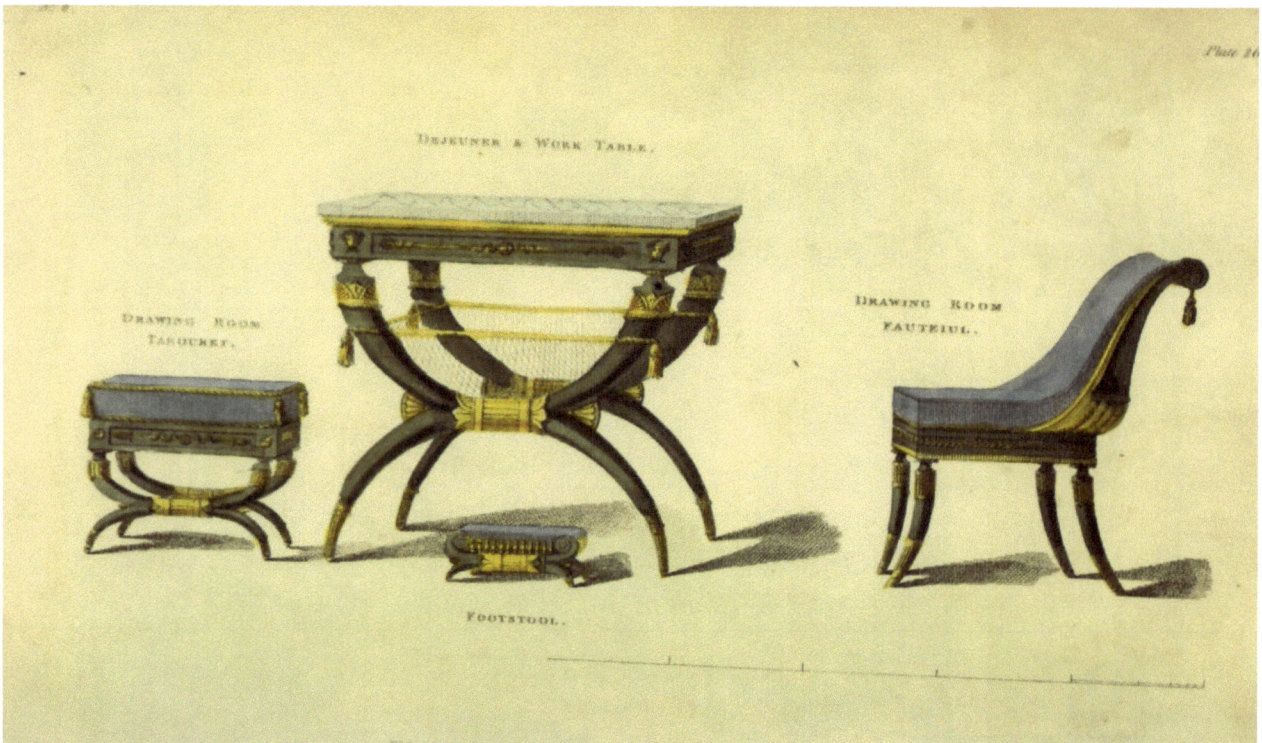

Dejeuner, or Work-Table
June 1809

DEJEUNER, OR WORK-TABLE

This elegant model for a table, designed and decorated after the Grecian style, is adapted for apartments of taste and superior elegance in their finishing. It should, in consequence, be executed in imitation of bronzed metal, the ornaments in burnished and matt-gold. A net-work, in gold-coloured silk, incloses the lower part, forming a bag for ladies' work and trinkets. The top of this table should be of some of the rarest and most beautiful species of marbles. The drawing-room, or boudoir, claims this elegant article of modem decoration, and which may with propriety be occasionally placed in the piers between the windows.

FOOTSTOOL

Under the above table we have placed a footstool, similar in its finishing and decoration. The covering should be of mazarine-blue velvet, with gold fringe on the fronts.

7

DRAWING-ROOM TABOURET

This article is designed in corresponding taste, and adapted to the work-table, having its frame as bronze, with the ornaments in or-moulu; the covering being of mazarine-blue velvet, with gold trimming and ornaments.

DRAWING-ROOM CHAIR

This chair should be similar in finishing to the preceding articles, viz. the ground-work of the frame in bronze, with the ornaments in gold or or-moulu; the covering of the scat and back in blue velvet, to suit the tabouret and footstool, trimmed with gold, and having a gold tassel attached to the scroll at the back.

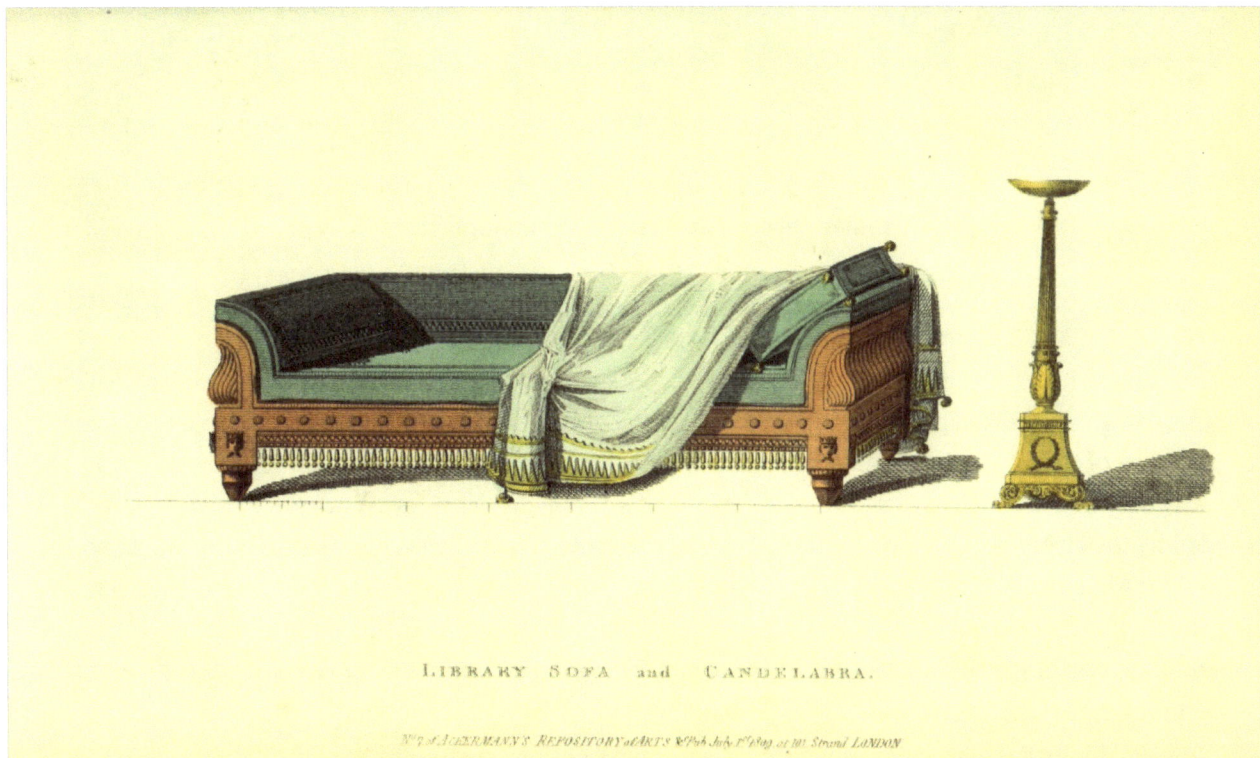

LIBRARY SOFA and CANDELABRA.

Library Sofa
July 1809

LIBRARY SOFA

Amongst the various decorations of a library, a sofa is an indispensible piece of furniture; it not only ornaments, but becomes a comfort when tired and fatigued with study, writing, and reading — the exhausted mind can only be recruited by occasional rest. The British artist is continually employing his ingenuity for comforts of the opulent, who, in return, liberally reward his exertions; and hence it is, that, in no other country in the world, is such completely convenience and comfort to be found as in England.

The annexed engraving represents a library sofa, with mahogany carved frame, Grecian small ends, French stuffed, bordered, and welted; covered with green Morocco leather, a square French bolster en suite, elegantly ornamented with rich Parisian fringe, a Chinese palampone, with handsome Vandyke border, tassels, &c. forming a light covering to draw over when reclined on.

Ladies Toilette, Fauteur and Footstool
August 1809

LADIES TOILETTE, FAUTEUR AND FOOTSTOOL

It cannot but be highly gratifying to every person of genuine taste, to observe the revolution which has, within these few years, taken place in the furniture and decorations of the apartments of people of fashion. In consequence of this revolution, effected principally by the study of the antique, and the refined notions of
beauty derived from that source, the barbarous Eyptian style, which a few years since prevailed, is succeeded by the classic elegance which characterized the most polished ages of Greece and Rome. In none of the articles of domestic convenience is this change more apparent, than in those which are subservient to the purposes of the toilet, which at once display the good taste of the fair owners, and the skill and ingenuity of the artists whom they patronize. This is strikingly exemplified in the appendages of the dressing-room represented in the annexed engraving.

The principal figure exhibits an elegant lady's toilet, a very handsome article, wrought in fine mahogany, superbly ornamented with highly finished brass, the center top folding back with a large-sized British plate glass. The interior is divided into various compartments, for every requisite for the accommodation of the accomplished female. Each end folding over, affords extra partitions and divisions, equally as necessary as the center. The whole is mounted on brass claw feet, with fret-work, of the same manufacture, encompassing the platform. In front of the toilet stands a convenient Ottoman footstool, French-stuffed, and covered with green Morocco leather, ornamented with brass-work en suite.

On the left is a fauteuil, with mahogany frame, French stuffed, and the seat covered with green Morocco leather, carved back, and brass ornaments.

On the right is placed a chamber-bath, which being of all others the most proper article for the promotion of health, more especially in the summer season, for either sex, it is impossible to recommend a more desirable piece of furniture.

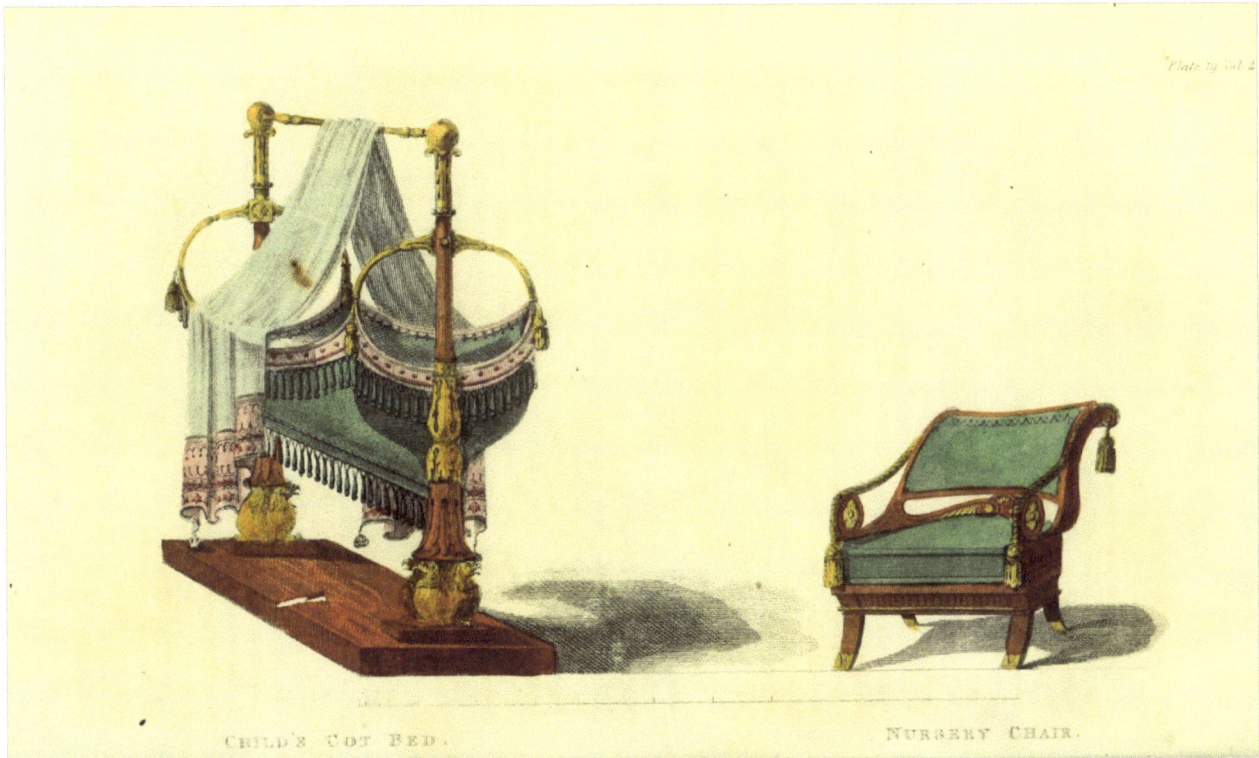

Child's Cot Bed & Nursery Chair
September 1809

CHILD'S COT BED & NURSERY CHAIR

Is the observations with which we prefaced the description of the furniture represented in our last number, we alluded to the surprising revolution which has, of late years, taken place in every article of domestic convenience or necessity in that line. This extraordinary improvement is no less strikingly illustrated by those elegant, ingenious, and commodious contrivances which have superseded the clumsy and noisy cradles, in which infants used to be rather jolted than soothed to sleep.

The annexed engraving exhibits a swing cot-bed for an infant, equally novel and elegant. This article may be completed in a plainer manner, or, as here represented, in a very handsome and superb style, standing on a mahogany base, the two uprights of mahogany, richly carved and gilded, supporting the swing cot, which moves with the greatest ease, and lulls the infant to sleep without the least noise. This is covered with green calico, rich silk, or satin, tastefully ornamented with Persian fringe, tassels, &c.

A simple throw-over furniture, en suite with the cover of the cot, bordered and fringed, is carelessly thrown over the top bearer, and regulated at pleasure. As a necessary appendage, is represented a Grecian nursery chair, in a mahogany carved frame, French stuffed, and covered with corresponding furniture to the cot-bed.

French Window Curtain & Grecian Settee
October 1809

The annexed engraving exhibits,

    1. An elegant French window-curtain, most tastefully ornamented with beautiful borders, rich Parisian fringe, lines, and tassels, suspended from two gilt rosettes (doing away the heavy effects of a cornice) amber colour, lined with French gray, or fine sky blue.

    2. A Grecian settee, or window-seat; the frame of mahogany, very neatly carved; seat French stuffed, and covered with morone leather, embossed border, printed on the edges, and fringed en suite with the drapery of the curtain; the back of mahogany open lattice work, carved, &c. corresponding with the other part of the frame. This tasteful article of furniture may be drawn from the window, to any other part of the room, not only affording the highest degree of comfort and convenience, but being also an elegant and fashionable ornament.

Drawing-Room Chairs
December 1809

DRAWING-ROOM CHAIRS

Drawing-room chairs are one of the most essential ornaments of the mansion and of the palace. The merchant, the nobleman, and the prince, are each vying with each other which shall excel in superb and elegant furniture. The annexed two drawings are specimens of very handsome chairs; the frame mahogany, richly carved, and gilt in burnished gold; the seat and back French stuffed, and quilted. They may be covered with the best red morocco leather, velvet, or (which is far more elegant) rich damask silk, ornamented with rich Persian fringe, and beautifully bordered en suite with the window-curtains.

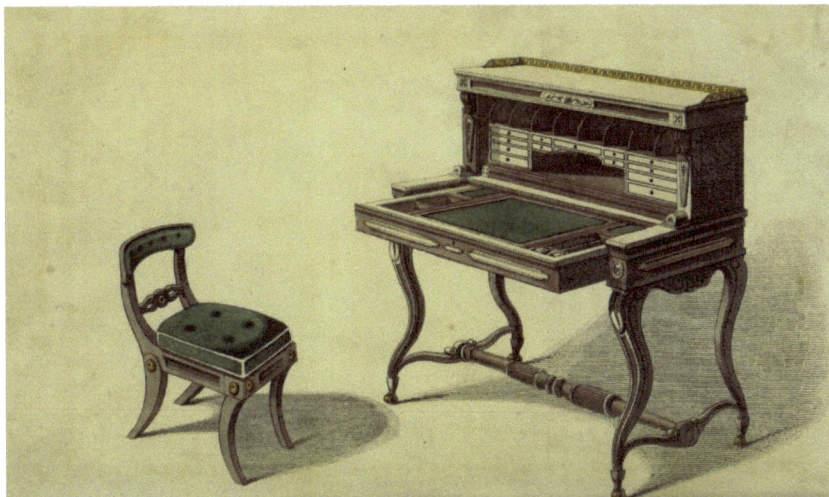

Cabinet Writing-Table
January 1810

CABINET WRITING-TABLE

The cabinet writing-table represented in the annexed engraving, is contrived on a new plan, forming at once an elegant piece of furniture and combining every possible convenience with the greatest simplicity. It is manufactured in mahogany, rose-wood, satin-wood, or the beautiful Brazil kingwood, &c. to any size. One lock secures the whole. By drawing out the desk, it disengages itself from the front, and by raising the front, which, by a simple contrivance, runs under the top, you come to the use of pigeon-holes and drawers.

Private drawers are made in the writing part, with ink and sand-glasses, &c.; the whole very handsomely carved and ornamented with bass or ivory. Beside it stands a very handsome and truly comfortable chair en suite, with a French cushion, and stuffed back.

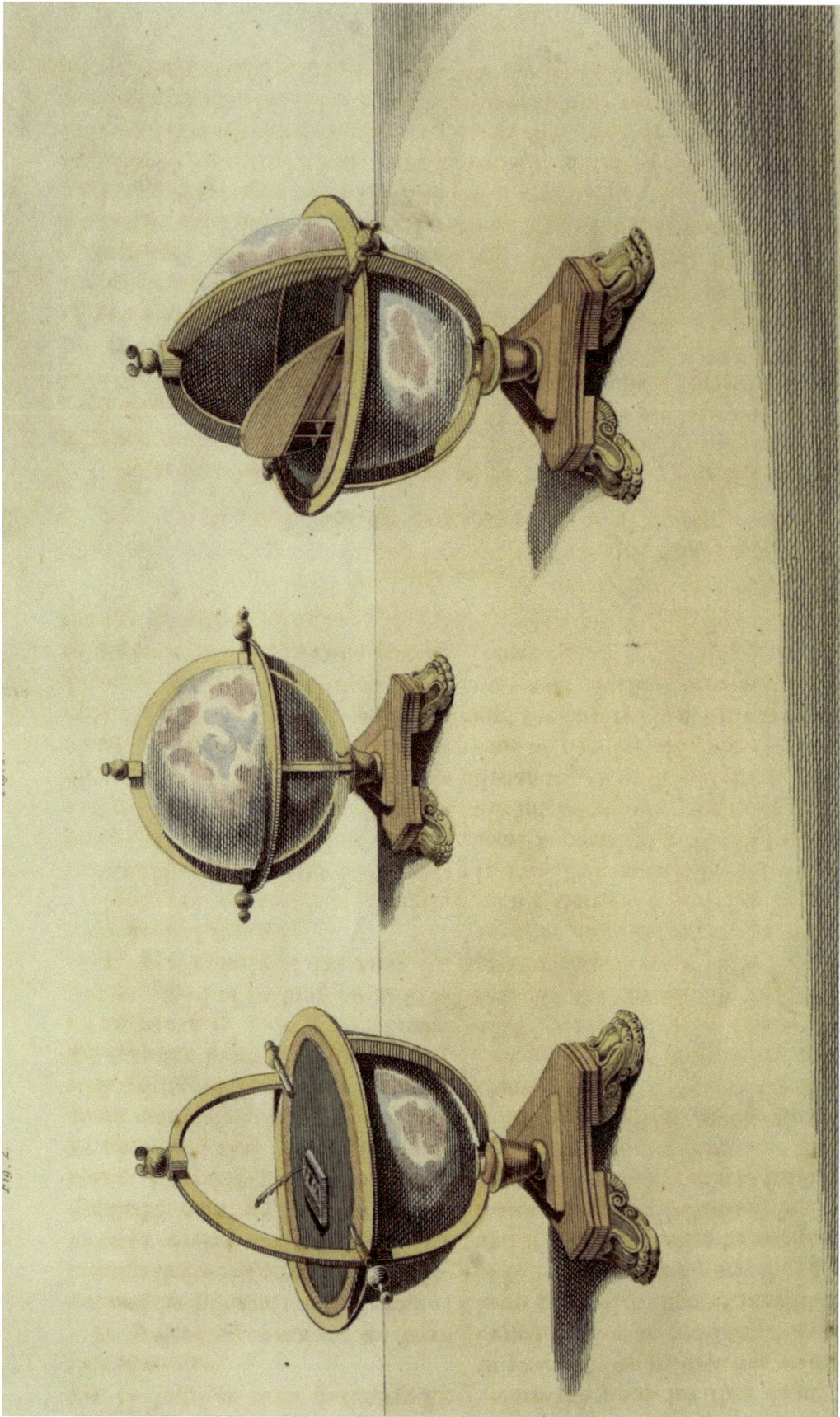

Pitt's Cabinet Globe Writing-Table
February 1810

PITT'S CABINET GLOBE WRITING-TABLE

Under this head we have had frequent occasion to remark on the high degree of ingenuity that has been for some years past displayed by British artists in the production of every article which either administers to our necessities, or contributes to our convenience. That which forms the subject of the annexed engraving furnishes an additional example of inventive talent. Pitt's Cabinet Globe Writing-Table, thus denominated as a humble tribute of respect to a late illustrious statesman, is of the grandest and most elegant pieces of furniture that ever decorated the modern library. It forms externally a handsome globe, which may be constructed of any size. In this form it represented in fig. 1.

In fig. 2. it is seen with two of the quarters let down, in which state it composes a circular writing-table. Fig. 3. shews the interior of the lower part fitted up with drawers, pigeon-holes, &c. for papers, and with only one quarter of the globe let down. The whole is secured by a patent lock, contrived in the ball at top.

This writing-table, which must be acknowledged equally convenient and superb, is likely to become an indispensable appendage to the library of every person of taste in the fashionable world. It has already obtained the patronage of her Majesty and Royal Family, who are the foremost to encourage real merit. Her Royal Highness the Princess Augusta has very recently ordered one of the inventors*, and it was from this that our drawings were made.

---

* Messrs. Morgan and Saunders, of Catherine-street, Strand.

Plate 15

Circular and Movable Book Case
March 1810

CIRCULAR AND MOVABLE BOOK CASE

The projector of this ingenious and elegant contrivance seems to have bad in recollection the conveniences afforded by the set of circular and movable tables formerly known by the appellation of dumb waiters. The application of this principle to the construction of a bookcase, is secured by a patent, under which Morgan and Sanders, of Catherine-street, Strand (in whose shew-rooms we observed it), manufacture the machine by permission. In construction it is thus arranged: Two circular shelves, placed about a foot apart, and inclosed in an appropriate frame and mounting, compose a cylindric* pedestal of 3 feet diameter and about 2 ½ feet high, on which is supported the superstructure of the movable part of the machine. This, in the present instance, consists of five shelves, progressively decreasing in diameter, and placed one above another in the order of their dimensions. Each shelf is furnished with a cover, corresponding shelf, at a distance above it, sufficient for the admission of the books it is intended to receive; and the two shelves thus situated are, with their contents, moved horizontally about an upright center, which passes through the whole machine. Small metal wheels or rollers, beneath the lower shelf, render this motion sufficiently easy for the hand, and at the same time ensure uniformity and steadiness. The upper side of this top shelf now forms a support for another pair of shelves, of smaller diameter, furnished also with rollers, and moving independent of the rest. This again affords a support for a third, of still smaller size; and thus the series is continued until the desired height, or number of shelves, is produced. The whole structure is surmounted with a vase, lamp, or other appropriate ornament, and the pedestal being furnished with substantial feet and rollers, the whole machine may with ease and security be wheeled by one person, to different parts of a room, or from one apartment to another.

This bookcase appears to afford some valuable conveniences, as, for instance, it may be placed in a recess, or in a corner of a room, in which, from local circumstances, it might be inconvenient or impossible to dispose the same number of books in straight lines, as in a common bookcase. The facility with which it may be moved, is, in many cases, also of considerable importance. It seems likewise to be entitled to a distinguished situation even in extensive libraries, where the volumes are already disposed in the usual way.

There are many occasions of literary research and reference, on which the floor and tables of the library are, from necessity, strewed with the works referred to: this circumstance is prevented, with all the consequent interruption and loss of time, by previously arranging the required volumes from the shelves of the library upon those of the machine, which may then be placed within reach of the right hand, and by a turn of the shelves afford immediate access to any volume it contains, without the necessity of quitting the seat. The cost is moderate, varying of course with the circumstances of ornamental and superior workmanship, which regulate the expence of other furniture.

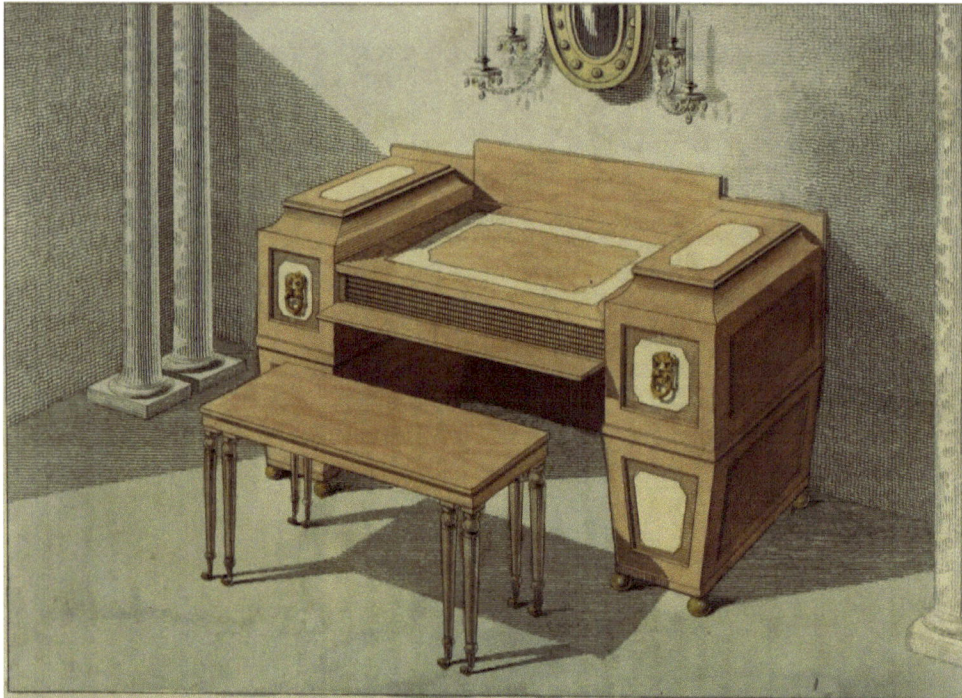

Patent Sideboard
April 1810

Patent Sideboard

The patent sideboard and dining-tables, constructed on the plan represented in our engraving, are universally allowed to be one of the most convenient as well as elegant pieces of furniture for the dining-room ever yet manufactured. They are as well calculated for small rooms as for the first nobleman's mansion, as they can be made from the smallest dimensions to the very largest size, and combine every possible convenience of a sideboard and table. The dining-tables, when not in use, may be shut within the sideboard; the extra flaps or leaves, are inclosed , as is shewn, in the middle top drawer; and the frame, which is made to draw out to any length for the support of the leaves, with the greatest possible ease, runs under the center of the sideboard, so that the whole forms, to appearance, only one piece of furniture.

These articles are made to any shape and plan, either to appear massy and solid, or light and elegant. The feet of the table are completely out of the way, so as not to annoy one person in sitting round the table. In this particular they far excel the claw tables, and are more firm and less complicated than any other kind of table whatever. They have already been made for many of the first mansions in the united kingdom , East and West Indies, Gibraltar, Spain, Portugal, Italy, Brazil, Sweden, and various parts of the Continent.

The first of these articles manufactured by the inventors, was ordered by the late Admiral Lord Nelson, for Merton-House. This circumstance induced the inventors to give them the name of Trafalgar patent dining-tables and sideboard. One advantage alone is sufficient to obtain them the preference before all others, that of clearing the hall and other parts of the house from lumber, as the whole of a table fifty or an hundred feet long, may, by this contrivance, be completely inclosed in the sideboard.

17

Roman Salon and Library Chairs
May 1810

ROMAN SALON AND LIBRARY CHAIRS

The first object of elegant antique furniture exhibits a specimen of the Roman chairs often placed in a saloon, or as extra chairs in a drawing-room or boudoir. They are either carved and gilt, or japanned, to suit other furniture; or in mahogany, with red morocco leather cushions, with a foot-stool en suite,

The library chair is often accommodated in the same way, and is allowed to be one of the most comfortable chairs now made. The Grecian footstool is also en suite, and by fixing a portable desk and candlestick with a shade, it forms a most complete chair for the study, dining-room, &c.

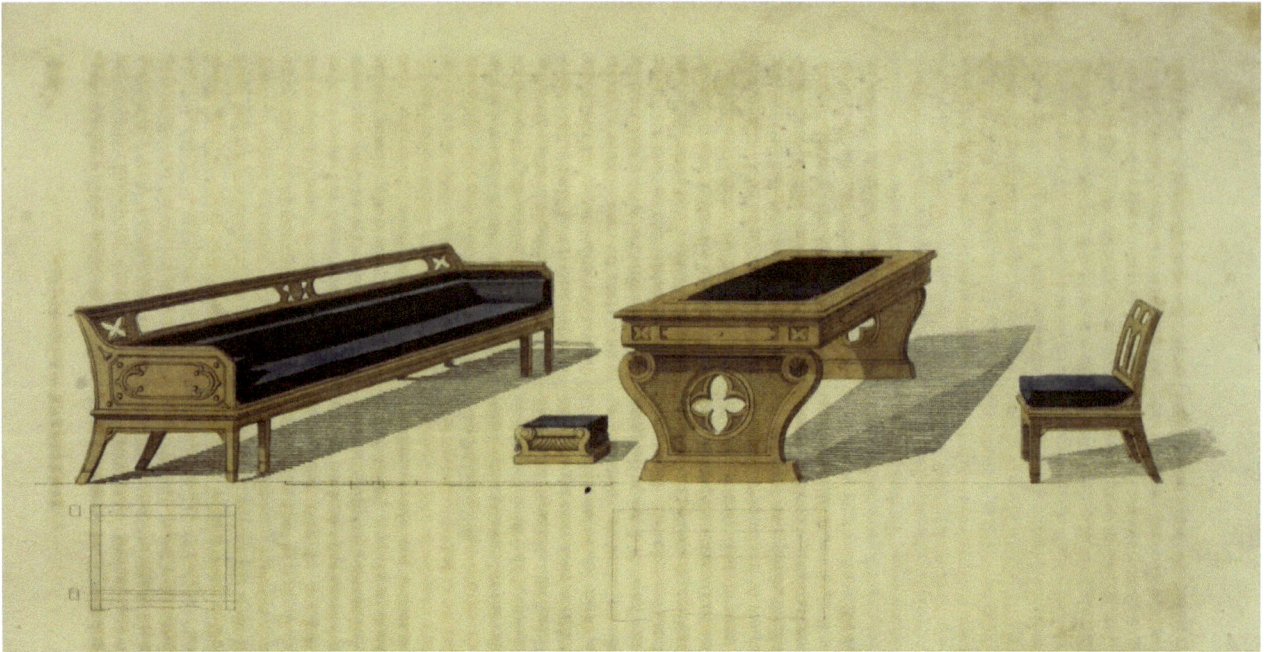

Gothic Sofa, Table, Chair and Footstool for a Library
June 1810

GOTHIC SOFA, TABLE, CHAIR AND FOOTSTOOL

Our engraving of furniture this month represents a handsome Gothic sofa table, chair, and footstool, adapted to a fashionable library. They are finished in the best manner in French stuffing morocco purple leather; and the frame, which may be either of mahogany, satin-wood, or wainscot, is supposed, in the specimen here exhibited, to be of the latter.

It may not be amiss to observe, that no person of a genuine taste will introduce articles in this style into his apartments, unless there be a general correspondence in the appearance of his house; otherwise a discordance is produced, which cannot fail to shock the eye of every spectator. By inattention to this principle, we have known individuals, of high reputation in matters of taste, absolutely fall into the grotesque and ridiculous. That such was the character of the residence of the late Mr. Walsh Porter, at Fulham, no connoisseur will be bold enough to deny. It seemed to be the study of this gentleman's life to crowd together into so small a compass every diversity of style, and imitations of the peculiar taste of every nation on the surface of the globe; and if he could not excite admiration, at least to keep the mind of the spectator in continual astonishment. An apartment, decorated with all the gaudy fineries of China, led you into a cavern, where you trembled lest you should encounter the dagger of some assassin; but having happily passed through without accident, you were ushered into a Turkish pavilion, which perhaps conducted you into a Gothic apartment, and that into a Grecian, &c. &c.; while a rustic public-house, whose characteristic accessories seemed to announce the recent departure of a company of boors from the scene of their carousal, served, instead of a porter's lodge, to introduce you to this motley mixture of extravagancies. — Such absurdities might afford pastime to youth, but are beneath the dignity of real taste; and persons of fortune, desirous of acquiring the reputation of possessing that quality, cannot be too careful to avoid them.

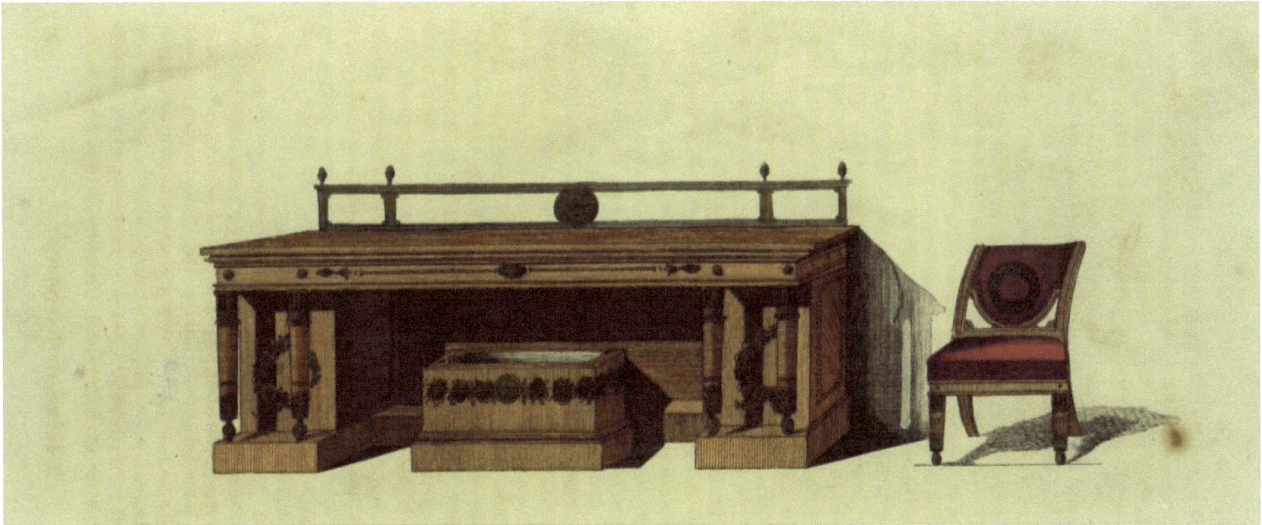

Sideboard & Dining-Room Chairs
July 1810

SIDEBOARD & DINING-ROOM CHAIRS

The accompanying representation of a sideboard and dining-room chair exhibits two articles of furniture well suited for a mansion or palace, grand and truly convenient. The former is fitted up with cellarets, wine-cooler, drawers, and other appendages, made of fine Jamaica mahogany, with bronze ornaments and back rail en suite. The chair is French -stuffed, seat and back covered with real Morocco leather. The space between the ends of the sideboard admits of a full -sized dining-table, frame, and leaves, at once preserving the table from injury, and clearing every part of the house from lumber.

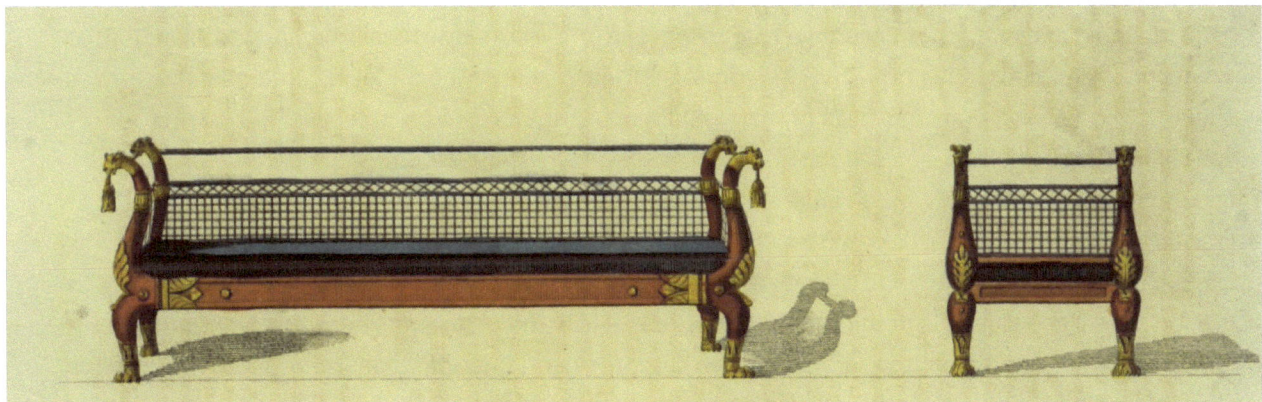

Sofa and Chair Banquettes
August 1810

SOFA AND CHAIR BANQUETTES

Our engraving of furniture this month represents two novel and elegant articles, suited for handsome, airy summer retreats, or any foreign climate, such as the East and West Indies, Gibraltar, &c.; saloons, and large apartments destined for grand entertainments. A suite of sofa and chair banquettes are articles of the first class for the mansions of the great and opulent. They may be made of mahogany, ornamented with brass, as represented in the plate; or in satin-wood, rose- wood, king's- wood, &c.; the seat French stuffed, and covered with morocco leather, satin, or silk; the back and ends of lattice or trellis-work, finished to correspond; or of silk cord, &c.; affording ail possible air and coolness for warm seasons and crowded assemblies.

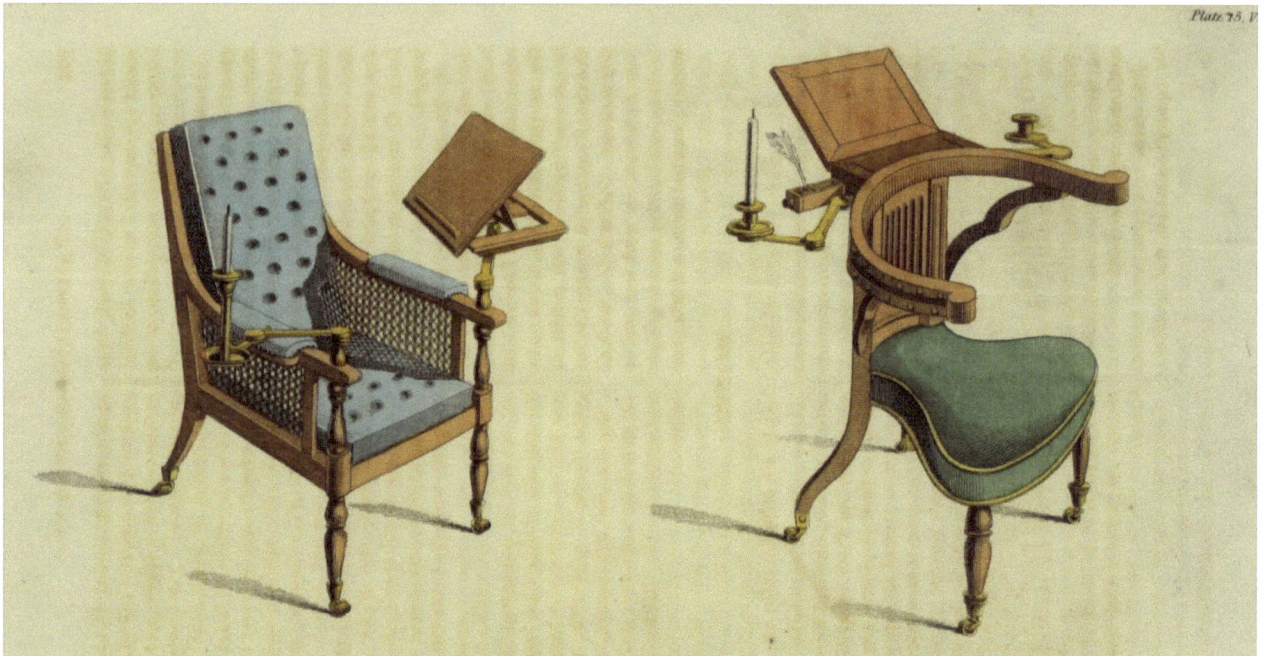

Library Reading Chairs
September 1810

Library Reading Chairs

Our engraving this month exhibits two of the most convenient and comfortable library chairs perhaps ever completed. Each of them has become a favourite piece of furniture for the library, boudoir, and, other apartments of the nobility and gentry. The first (on the left-hand side of the plate) is made of mahogany, or any other wood; the back, seat, and sides caned, with French stuffed cushions and covers; the arms corresponding; a movable desk and candlestick, affording every possible accommodation for reading, writing, &c. The whole chair is of itself completely comfortable.

The second is a more novel article, but equally convenient and pleasant: gentlemen either sit cross, with the face towards the desk, contrived for reading, writing, &c. and which, by a rising rack, can be elevated at pleasure; or, when its occupier is tired of the first position, it is with the greatest ease turned round in a brass grove, to either one side or the other; in which case, the gentleman sits sideways. The circling arms in either way form a pleasant easy back, and also, in every direction, supports for the arms. As a proof of their real comfort and convenience, they are now in great sale at the ware-rooms of the inventors, Messrs. Morgan and Saunders, Catherine-street, Strand.

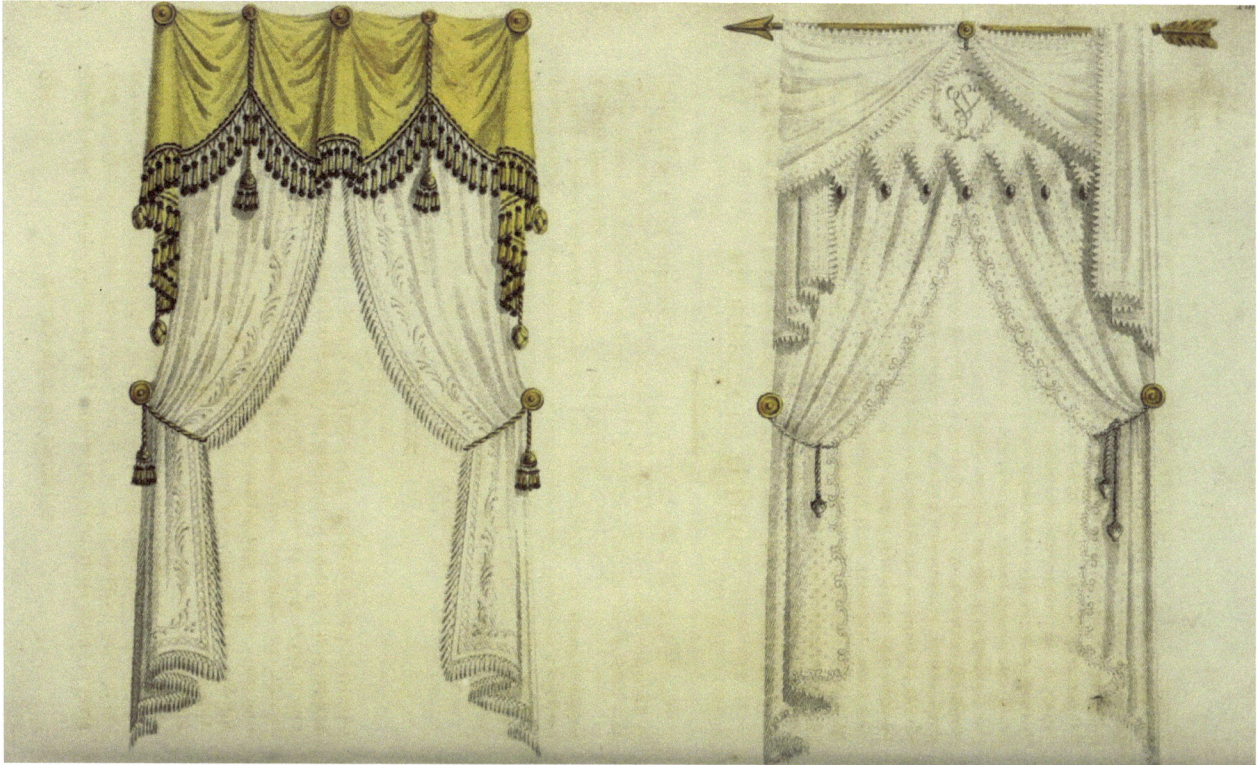

French drapery window-curtains
October 1810

FRENCH DRAPERY WINDOW-CURTAINS

The two beautiful French drapery window-curtains represented in our engraving, are patterns of a style at once elegant and simple: the yellow drapery of the first is made of lemon-coloured silk, hanging from large rosette pins, instead of a cornice, handsomely ornamented with silk cord and fringe; the curtains (drawing on a rod underneath) are of curiously embroidered muslin, beautifully bordered and fringed en suite. The other curtain is equally elegant, the drapery being simply hung over a gilt dart, and composed of fine spotted muslin, fringed.

Both these curtains and drapery may be made of chintz cotton, according to choice, as well as of silk or muslin.

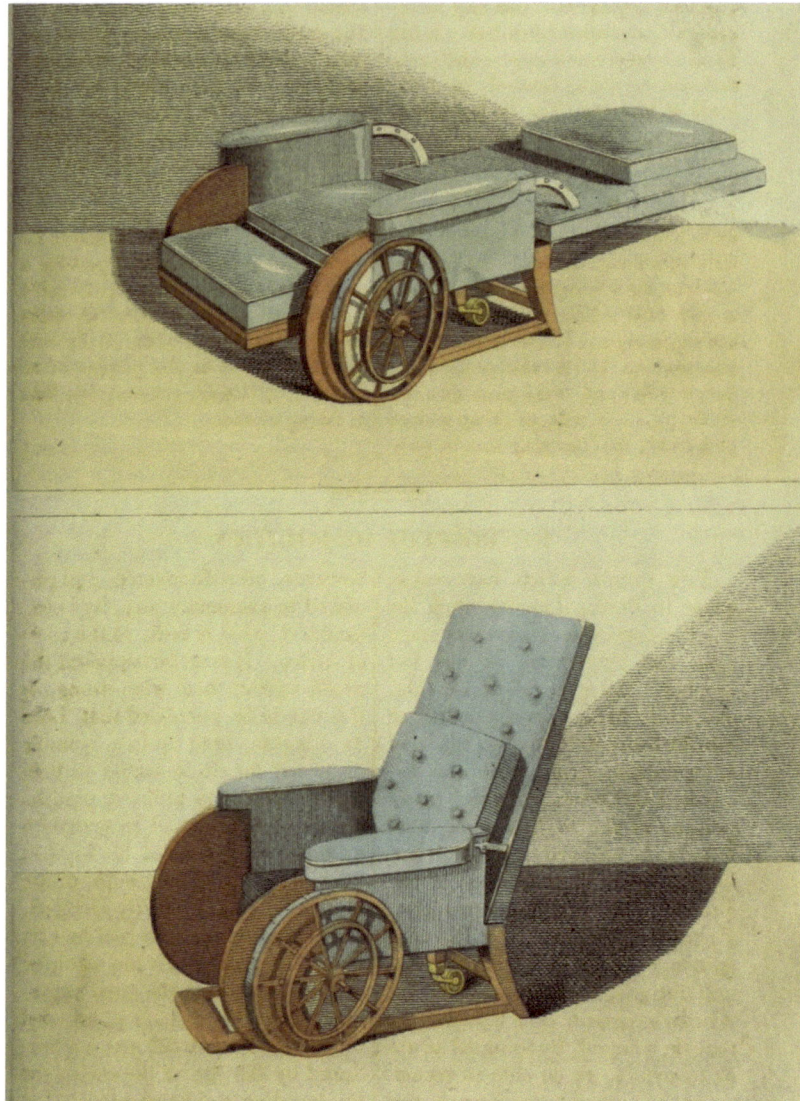
Invalid Chair and Sliding Stool
November 1810

INVALID CHAIR AND SLIDING STOOL

The engraving which accompanies this article, represents a highly approved and ingenious invalid chair, that may be occasionally converted into a bed. It first forms a most comfortable arm-chair; underneath is a sliding footstool, which extends at pleasure. The back slopes to any elevation, which is regulated by two strong iron quadrants and pins, rising or falling to any distance. The back at last falls quite flat and level with the seat; immediately under which there is also a slide that draws out, and becomes level also with the seat and back. The whole is then of a sufficient length for a bed; and supposing a person so ill as not to be able to sit up, by the assistance of a pillow it will wheel to any place required. If the patient is able to sit up and use both hands, the chair may then be guided either in a room, or any part of a house, lawn, street, road, or pleasure-ground, with the greatest ease and safety. The smaller inside mahogany wheels are parts by which the two hands are to steer the chair; the large wheels are shod with iron, and thus prepared for gravel walks, &c. The frame is mahogany, stuffed in canvas with the best curled hair, covered either with leather, chintz cotton, or other materials. The whole forms a very handsome piece of furniture for any apartment whatever, and perhaps a more desirable article was never invented for aged persons or invalids. — A dome canopy may also be added to fit over the head, answering the purpose of an umbrella or parasol, either against heat or falling weather.

Sideboard
December 1810

SIDEBOARD

The accompanying engraving exhibits a representation of a sideboard, constructed on a plan of peculiar utility, with truly convenient cellaret drawers and cupboards inclosed within each pedestal, having two small drawers above, with a pair of handsome vase knife-cases, and the center may form two drawers, or one long drawer, to receive extra loose flaps of the dining-table, while the frame of the table runs underneath on castors. The front of this side-board is of handsome mahogany, inlaid with various beautiful woods, and curious lacquered brass work. The shape and size may be adapted to any other furniture in the room, and varied according to fancy and taste. Sideboards on this plan are made at Messrs. Morgan and Sanders's manufactory, Catharine-street, Strand.

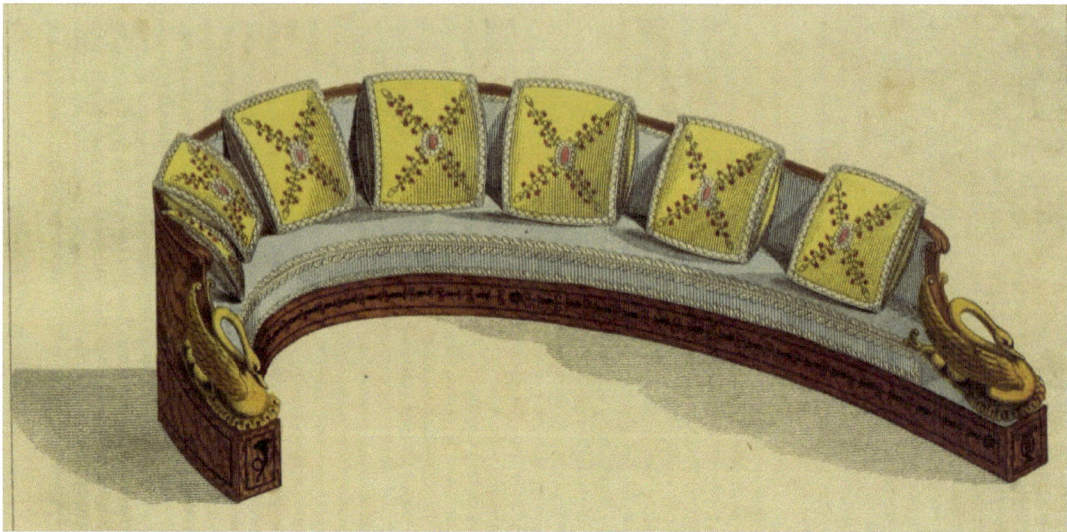
Imperial Turnkey Ottoman or Circular Sofa
January 1811

IMPERIAL TURNKEY OTTOMAN OR CIRCULAR SOFA

We are of opinion, that a more elegant article of furniture never graced the drawing-room of a prince, than the circular ottoman, or sofa, represented in the annexed engraving. The frame is made of curious Brazil zebra wood, most beautifully inlaid, and ornamented with brass, or-molu, and bronze. The king-wood, rose-wood, or mahogany, would be equally proper, provided the other furniture corresponds. The two swans are carved out of the solid wood, richly glided, and shaded with bronze; the seat and back French stuffed, as are also the swans and loose cushion, and covered with damask satin silk, most superbly embroidered edged, and ornamented. For a bow- window, or a room with a circular end, a more elegant piece of furniture cannot be introduced. This superb article is the production of the manufactory of Morgan and Sander, Catherine-street, Strand.

Drawing Room Chairs
February 1811

DRAWING ROOM CHAIRS

For drawing-rooms of handsome dimensions, a more appropriate and superb article cannot possibly be introduced to the notice of the public, than the chairs represented in our engraving for the present month. The frames of these elegant drawing-room chairs are richly carved, with burnished gold and green bronze; the seat and backs French stuffed; and they are covered with beautiful embroidered satin. The latter most of course be en suite with the window curtains, and of any colour suited to the taste of fancy of the purchaser.

25

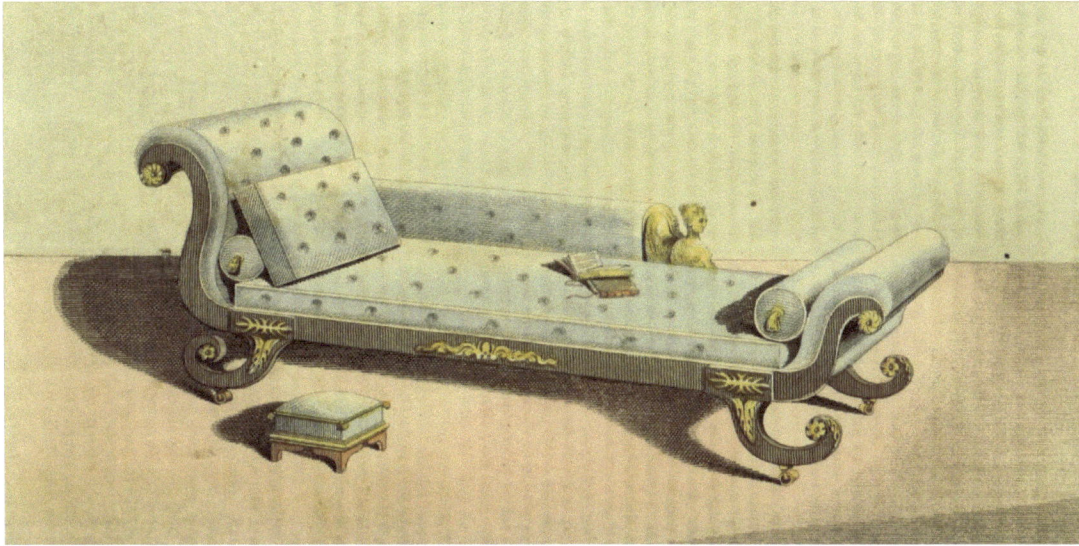

Library Couch
March 1811

LIBRARY COUCH

A very elegant Grecian sofa, adapted for the library, boudoir, or any fashionable apartment; the frame either in mahogany, ornamented with or-molu, or rosewood, &c.; the squab, &c. French stuffed, with bolsters and cushions covered with green morocco leather, stuffed with silk. Any other colour, or either chintz or silk damask, may be applied as covers.

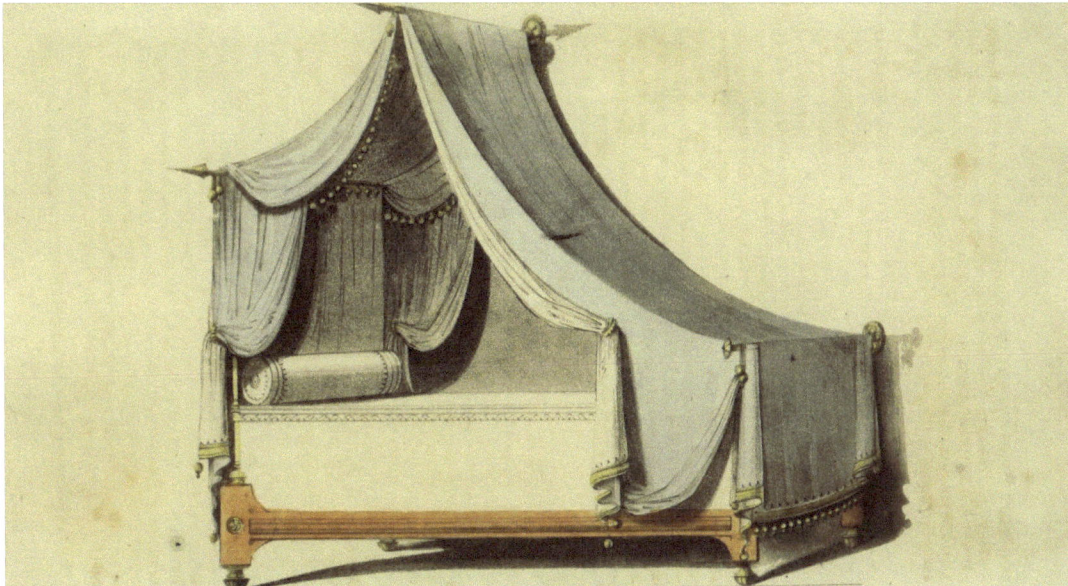

Military Couch-Bed
April 1811

MILITARY COUCH-BED

The military couch-bed, represented in our engraving, forms two elegant pieces of furniture, both, useful and ornamental, and cannot but be a most desirable article for every family of distinction. A couch-bed on this plan, which may be made almost in a thousand different forms, and in any style of fashion, is one of the most complete accommodations it is possible for an upholsterer to invent, for a second drawing-room, dressing-room, &c. A further description is scarcely necessary, the drawing explains itself: it may be made highly ornamental, or id a more plain and neat manner.

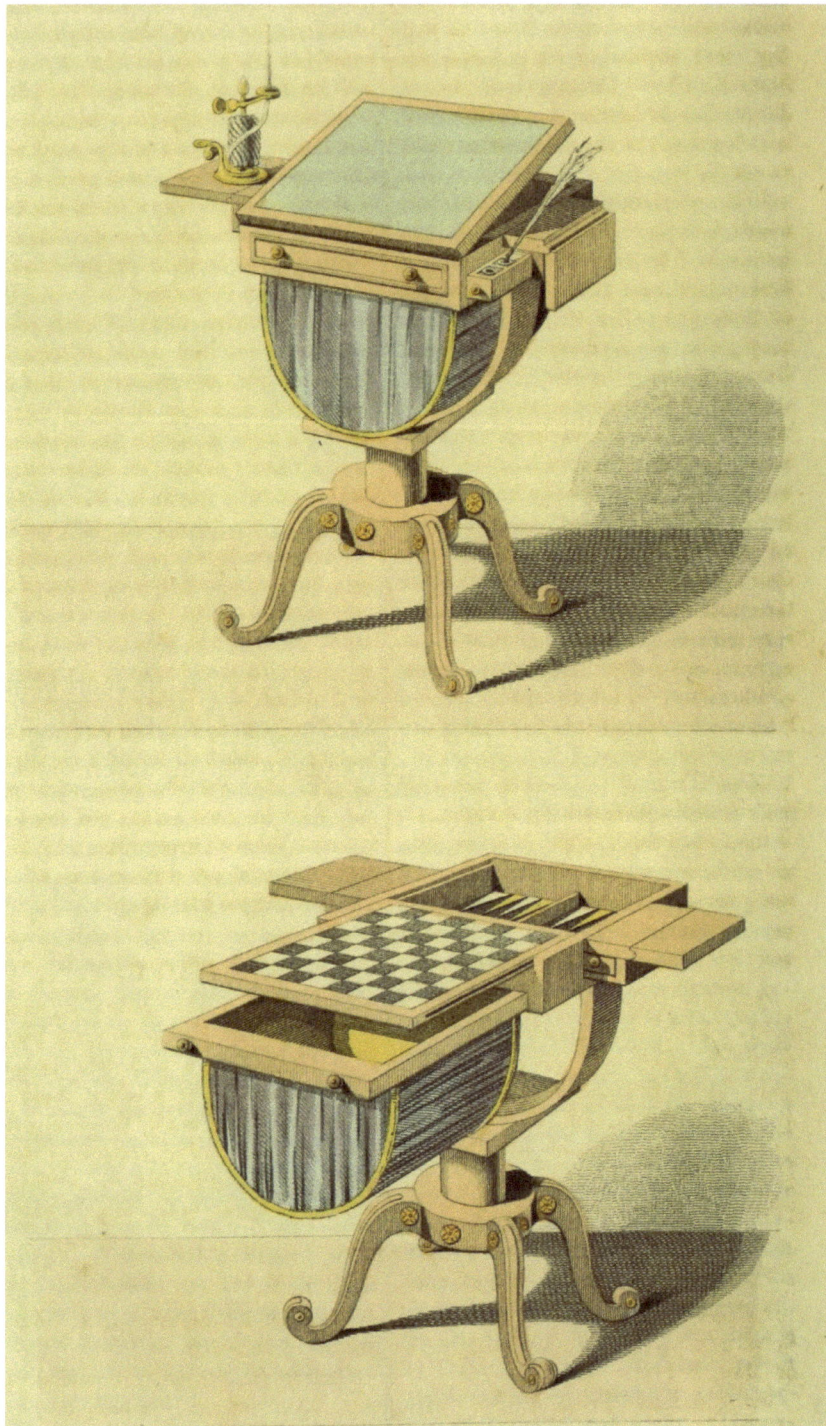

Lady's Work-Table
June 1811

LADY'S WORK-TABLE

   Our engraving this month represents a lady's backgammon work-table, comprehending seven different accommodations. In the first place, a very elegant and ornamental piece of furniture for a drawing room or boudoir, or a convenient reading and writing table, with ink, pens, &c. By sliding the desk off, it then forms a back-gammon, chess, and draft table. Underneath is a handsome silk bag for a work-bag, or any other purpose. The whole is made of fashionable Brazil wood, beautifully inlaid, and ornamented with or-moulu brass. Morgan and Sanders are the inventors and manufacturers of this elegant article.

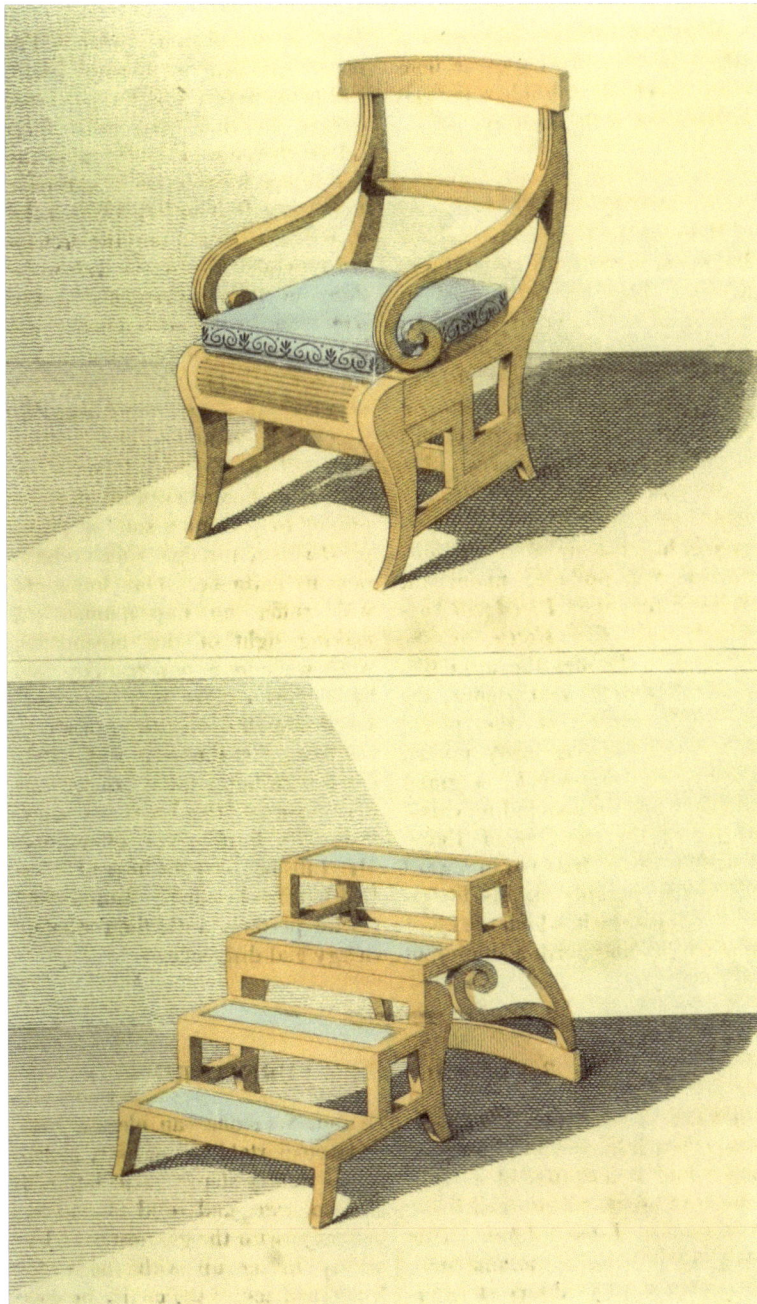

Metamorphic Library Chair
July 1811

METAMORPHIC LIBRARY CHAIR

Under this head, we this month present our readers with a representation and description of a truly novel and useful article, called the Metamorphic Library Chair. This chair, which forms, at the same time, a complete set of library steps, is considered the best and handsomest article ever yet invented, where two complete pieces of furniture are combined in one — an elegant and truly comfortable arm-chair, and a set of library steps. The latter is as firm, safe, and solid as a rock, and may, with the greatest ease, by merely lifting up with the right hand the back of the chair, be metamorphosed info as complete an arm-chair as can be wished for. It may be made of mahogany, or any other wood, and to any shape or size, either as represented in the plate, or with caned back and sides, and French stuffed cushions covered with Morocco leather, &c. This ingenious piece of furniture is manufactured at Messrs. Morgan and Saunders's, Catherine-St. Strand.

28

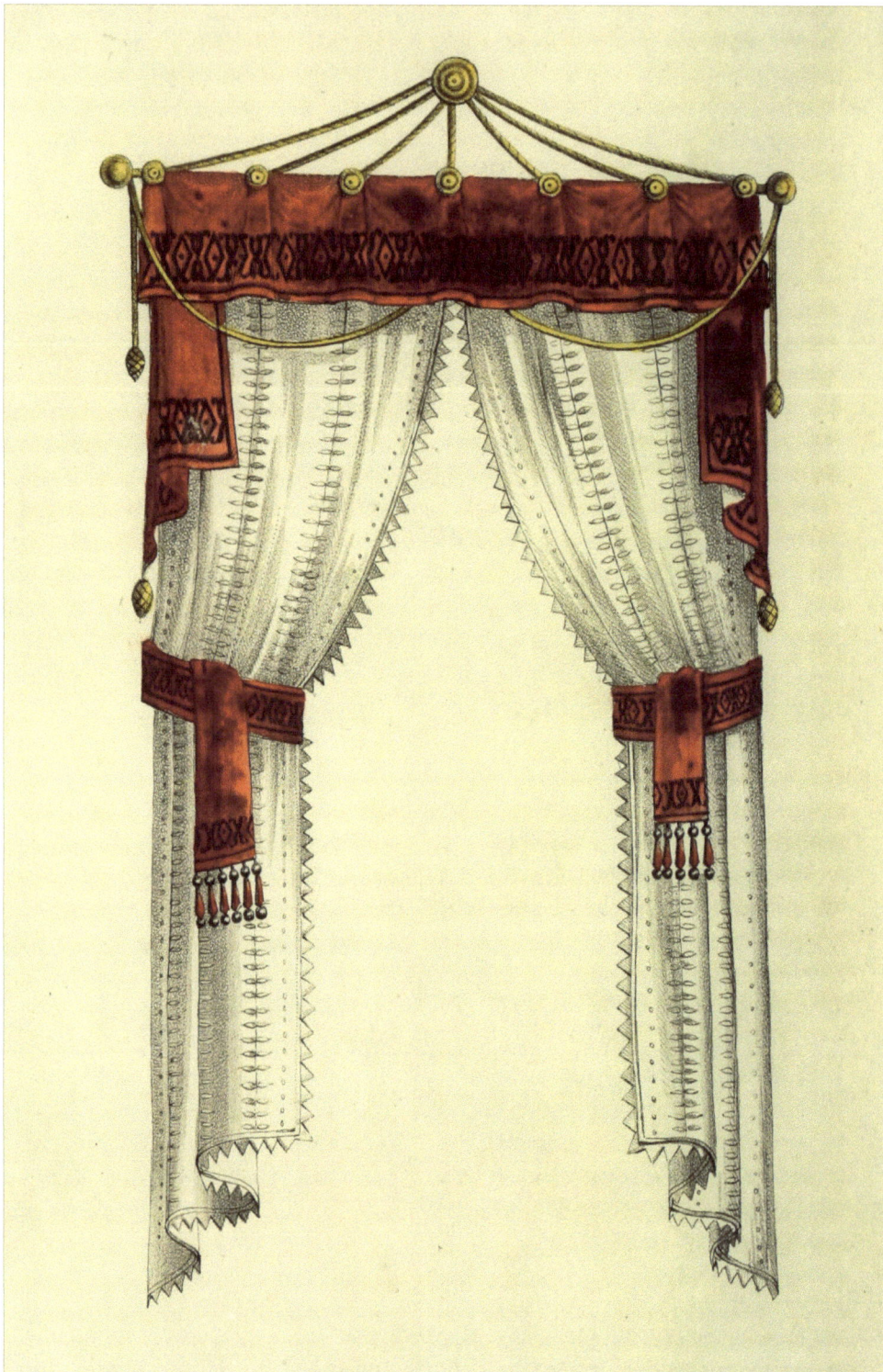

French Window-Curtain
August 1811

FRENCH WINDOW-CURTAIN

    A beautiful military belt drapery window-curtain, slung from a naval clue and lines, either of morine or kerseymere cloth, with rich embossed border, and fringed; the curtain of vandyke muslin, displaying a simplicity and elegance superlatively pleasing.

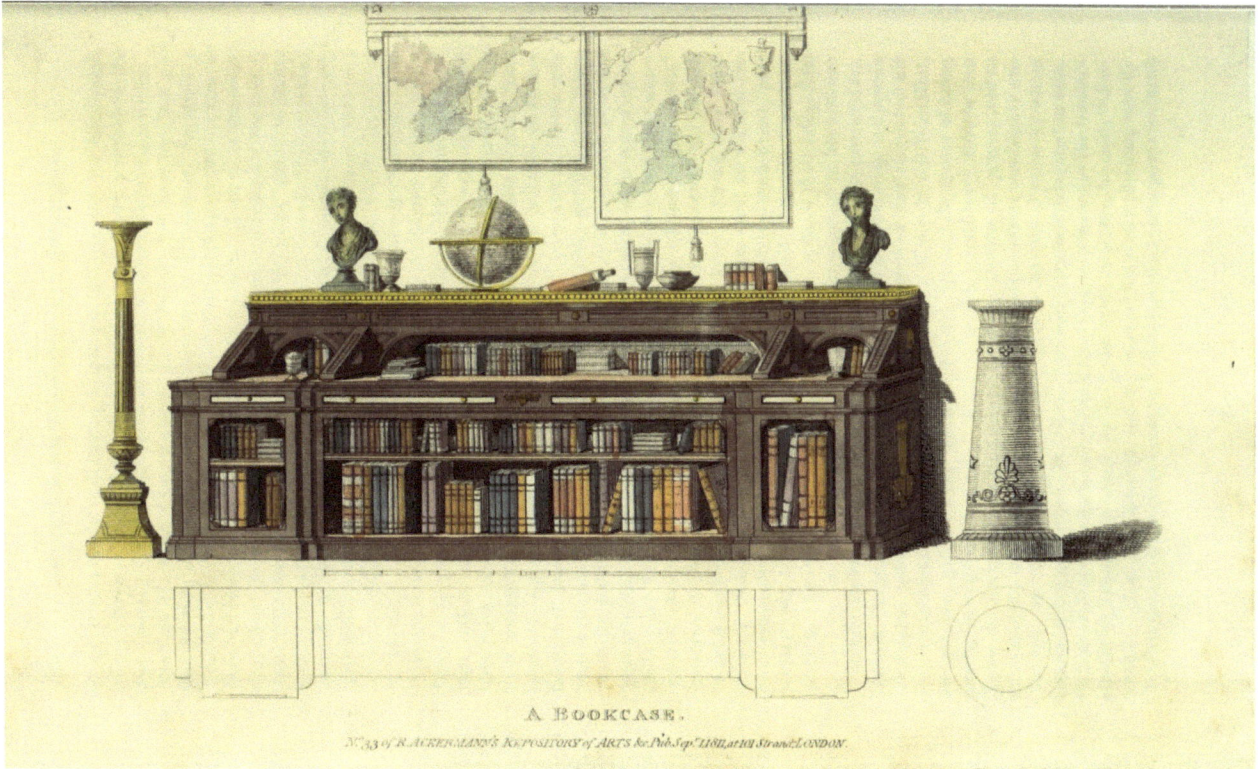

Dwarf Library Bookcase
September 1811

DWARF LIBRARY BOOKCASE

The annexed engraving represents a fashionable dwarf library bookcase, made of mahogany; the shelf ornamented with brass fret-work, shallowed off for small books, &c; the under parts being made deep in proportion for larger books; standing on a plinth; the whole beautifully ornamented with various woods and brass work. Immediately under the upper row of books are four slides, with brass knobs to draw them out, each forming a desk, &c. The front view is a pedestal break, with arched top shelves, the two ends being deeper than the center. The globe vases, telescope, &c. &c. with busts of Milton and Newton, crown the whole. The pedestal on the right, and the candelabrum on the left, are appendages peculiarly convenient, as well as ornamental.

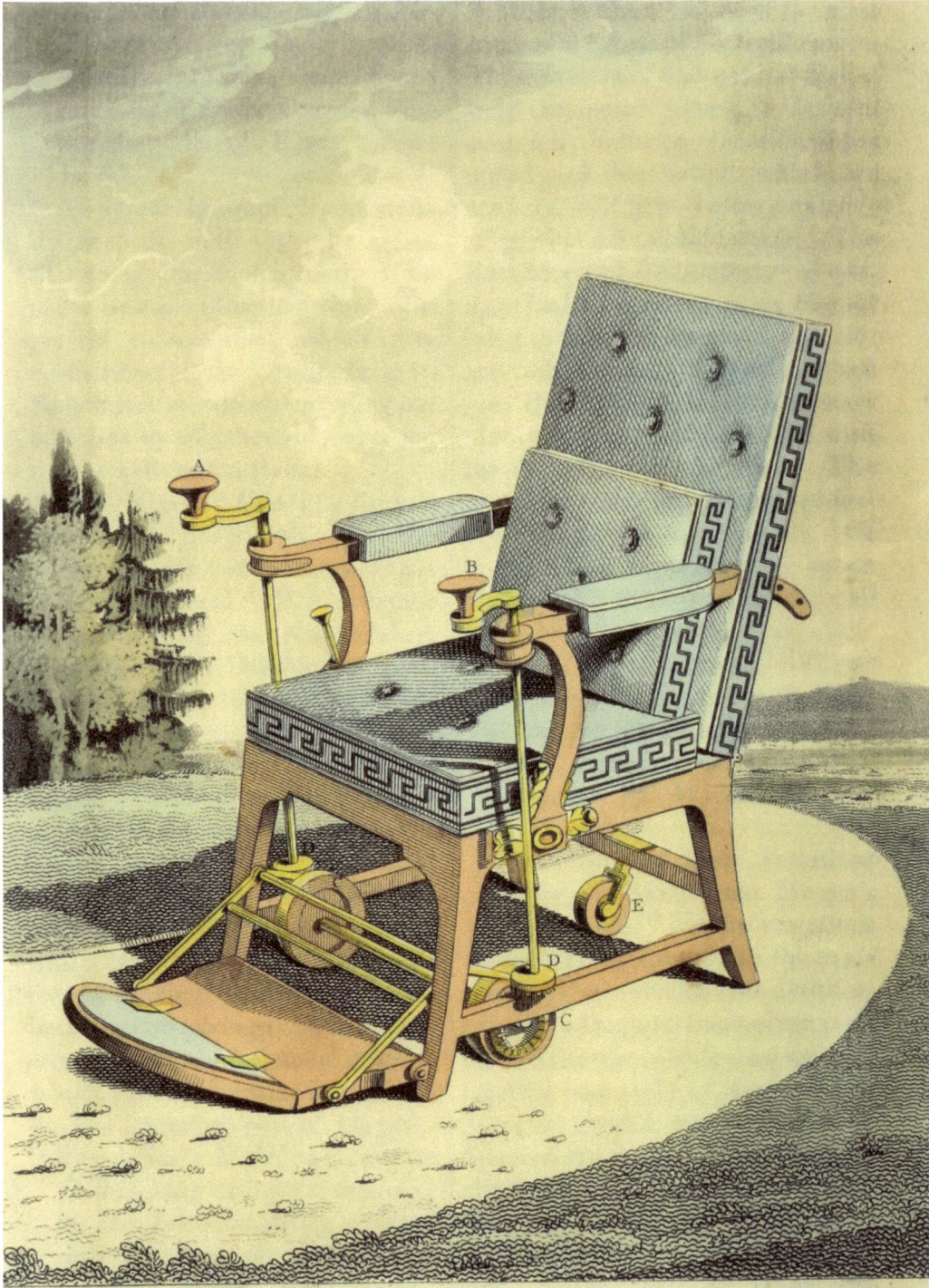

Merlin's Mechanical Chair
October 1811

MERLIN'S MECHANICAL CHAIR

This curious machine, of which a correct perspective view is given in the annexed engraving, is the contrivance of the late ingenious and well-known Merlin. It is expressly calculated for the accommodation of invalids who, from age or infirmity, are unable to walk about, or of persons, under the temporary inconvenience of gout or lameness.

In the library, or on the lawn, or gravel-walk of the pleasure-ground, chairs of this kind are peculiarly useful and pleasant. They are in construction an easy reclining or arm-chair, with a foot-board, and, at the extremity of each arm, a small winch handle, easily turned by the hands of the person seated, and which, by their connection with an arrangement of wheels below, propel the chair in any required direction, or with any required velocity, at the pleasure of the operator. These operating handles are seen in the drawing at A and B. CC are two wheels on which the chair runs, having each on its flat and outer surface a brass face wheel, worked by a smaller one (marked D) fitted on the long axis of the winch handle.

E is a third wheel or castor, fitted to the back rail of the chair, and which forms a third point of support, and obeys the direction taken by the wheels CC.

The mode of operation is this: The party being seated, the small brass rod seen in the drawing, passing through the right-hand arm of the chair, is pulled upwards a little way to disengage the wheels, and the winch handle set to point forward as in the position represented in the drawing.

Now, if the two handles be both turned outwards the chair moves directly forward. If turned inwards it moves directly backwards. If the right-hand winch be turned outwards, the left remaining at rest, the chair turns sharply to the left, moving on its left wheel as a center; and vice versa of the left-hand winch if turned the same way, or of the right-hand one if turned inwards or the contrary way. If the two handles be turned the same way, i. e. both to the right-hand, or both to the left, at the same time, the chair will move sharply round to the right or left, having its center, or the operator himself, as its center.

The curious evolutions which may thus easily be performed in this chair render it the means of very considerable amusement, as well as of important use, to those who require its agency; but to the mechanical observer it possesses a new interest. It would not be difficult to contrive an arrangement for moving these wheels, or winch handles, by the action of a very small and portable steam-engine, and increasing the dimensions of the whole machine, and adapting to it a suitable upper structure, to render it a most curious mode of quick conveyance, without the agency of animal labour: indeed, it seems to require no great stretch of the imagination to form of the contrivance many other highly interesting machines.

A suitable construction might be hit upon to enable it to carry a small cannon, which should be, both for itself and its operators, completely unassailable by the enemy, as well as, by the singular rapidity of its evolutions, terribly and unusually destructive.

In judicious hands, the principle of the machine might possibly be advantageously used in the construction of a self-moving engine for the public conveyance of dispatches, which would have for its leading peculiarities, a rapid and certain rate of travelling, and complete inviolability as to the matters entrusted to its charge.

Of the interest and value of the contrivance in its present shape, those only can judge correctly who have experienced its singular advantages.

This drawing is furnished us by Messrs. Morgan and Sanders, of Catherine-street, Strand, whose warehouses are the grand emporium for furniture combining all the essentials of elegance and comfort.

French Window-Curtains
November 1811

FRENCH WINDOW-CURTAINS

The annexed sot of drapery French window-curtains, displays a style of hanging drawing-room curtains, and combining solid elegance with richness of fancy: of course, the colours and quality are left to choice and kind of situation. Bronze and gold ornaments, and poles, may also be regulated to colours, &c. The Regent's plume of feathers is very elegant and ornamental. — A French curtain is so well known, and the drawing itself so completely explains every particular, that it is needless to expatiate any further on the subject.

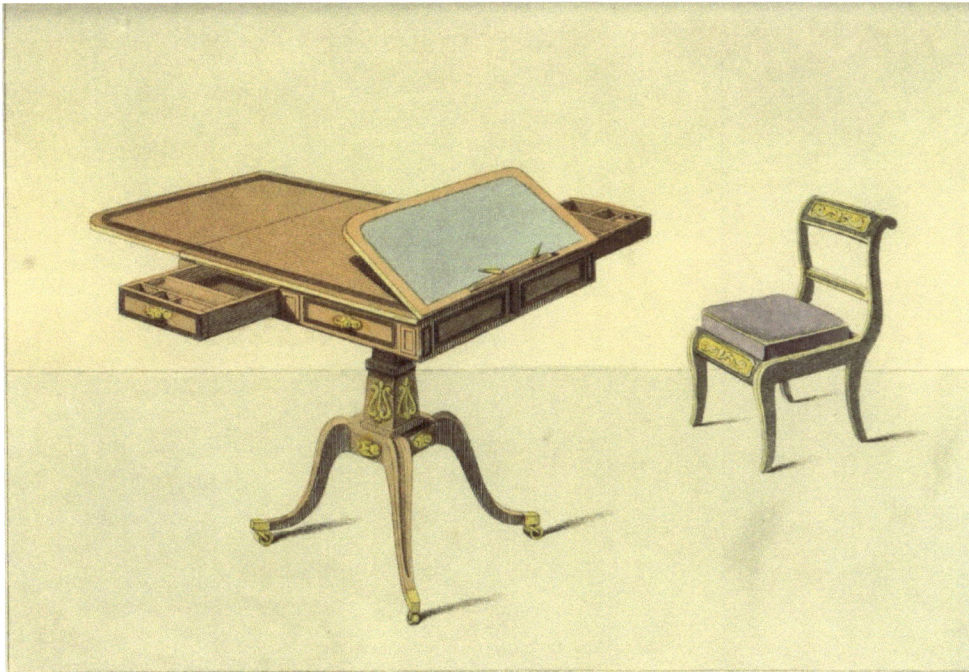

Sofa Writing-Table
December 1811

SOFA WRITING-TABLE

The annexed engraving, of a new-invented sofa writing-table, represents one of the most simple and useful articles it is possible to have in the drawing-room, boudoir, or any apartment for the accommodation of ladies. It forms, in the first place, a handsome small card- table, and, with the help of two sloped neat pieces of mahogany or other wood, it becomes two writing or reading tables, having one drawer in each side, fitted up with pen, ink, and paper, so that two persons may at one time use it either as a writing or reading table, neither being able to overlook the other.

By drawing out at each end the ornamented brackets, for the support of the two end flaps, it then forms as handsome a sofa table as can possibly be contrived either of mahogany, satin-wood, rose, king, or any other fashionable Brazil wood.

The fashionable Trafalgar chair, with a French stuffed cushion, accompanying the table, speaks for itself.

Four Posted Bed
January 1812

FOUR POSTED BED

   The superb bed, of which we give a perspective view, resembles, in its general features and construction, a very handsome state bed lately built for the Marquis of Winchester. The artist has, however, omitted in his drawing the introduction of the armorial crest, and similar local ornaments of that bed; and has introduced other tasteful decorations, and has introduced other tasteful decorations, which render it certainly more elegant in its appearance, and give the mass a more decided and picturesque effect: this may, therefore, be considered rather an original design, than a mere portrait. The present prevailing ornament of the Regent's plume is here new, and the cornices are perforated for the admission of the draperies, instead of having them twisted round or over them. We trust that this, with other designs and views of elegant furniture given in this work, may tend to increase the practice of consulting the studies of artists in the choice and arrangement of those articles; and that our upholsterers, who are in general themselves men of enlightened taste, as well as excellent mechanics, will, with such aid (which their opportunities can rarely allow them time to cultivate themselves), render the household furniture of British manufacture as celebrated for its style of design, as it so justly is for its excellence of workmanship.

Cabinet Piano-Forte
February 1812

CABINET PIANO-FORTE

The general approbation of piano-fortes, as instruments of refined entertainment, and the elegance with which they are finished, in the different manufactories of the metropolis, have long rendered them an indispensable article for apartments, furnished, as well in the simplest, as in the most costly style. This being the case, we cannot be charged with any impropriety in selecting one of these instruments as the subject of our engraving for this department of our present Number.

The cabinet piano-forte, represented in the print, is a specimen chosen from among the extensive variety composing the stock of Messrs. Wilkinson and Wornum, whose improvements have procured it a very high degree of reputation, so that it is now becoming an article of general and fashionable request. It is an instrument of much elegance, with the usual additional keys and pedals. Its height varies from six to seven feet two inches; its width is three feet eight or nine inches; and its projection twenty- one inches. For touch, it is unrivalled, and in its adaptation to the voice, it is extremely happy, particularly that with two unisons or strings to one note. Instruments of this kind, finished in mahogany, are highly ornamental, but if in rose-wood and brass, they may be pronounced truly superb. They may be inspected, finished in various ways, at the manufactory of Messrs. Wilkinson and Wornum, 315, Oxford-street.

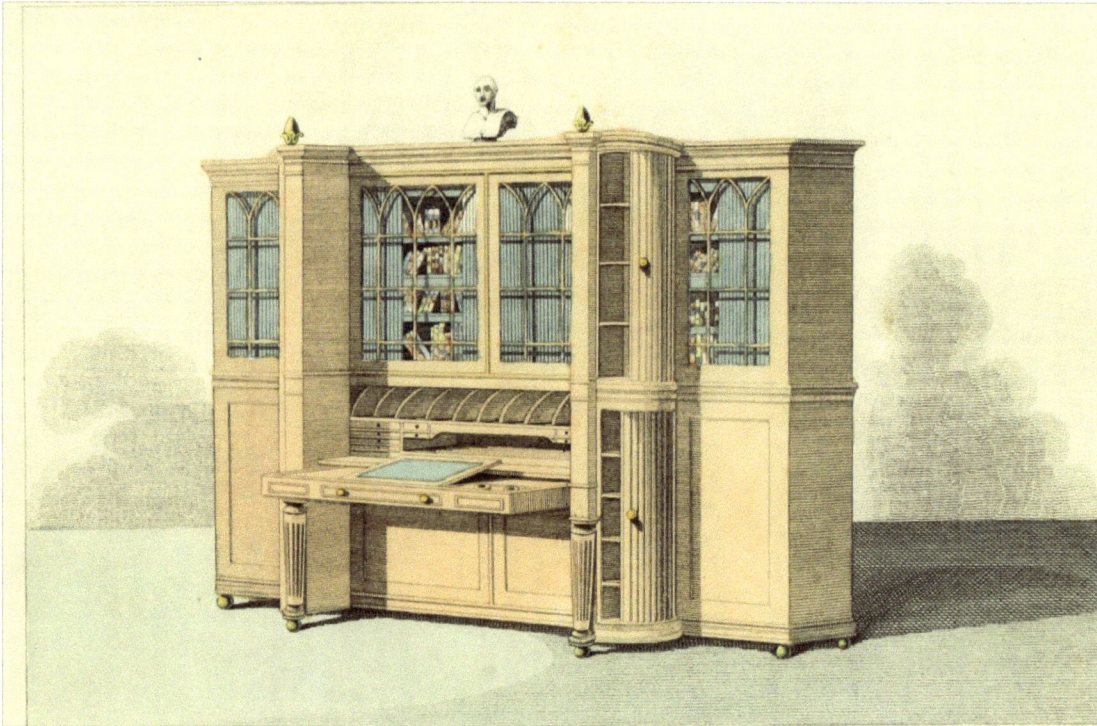

Library Bookcase
March 1812

LIBRARY BOOKCASE

The annexed engraving represents a wing tambour bookcase of quite a new pattern. Each end is fitted up with shifting shelves grooved, glazed doors, and cupboards. The tambour circular cupboards give a new effect, and are very ornamental as well as useful: the center between them is as usual for books, with glazed doors, &c.; under which is a perfectly new invention, drawing out and forming a complete writing-table, at least four feet wide, the top part running back, shewing the pigeon-holes, drawers, &c. under which are cupboards. It is presumed a more complete article of the kind cannot be had for the library, &c. It is made of mahogany, or any other wood, by Messrs. Morgan and Sanders, Catharine-street.

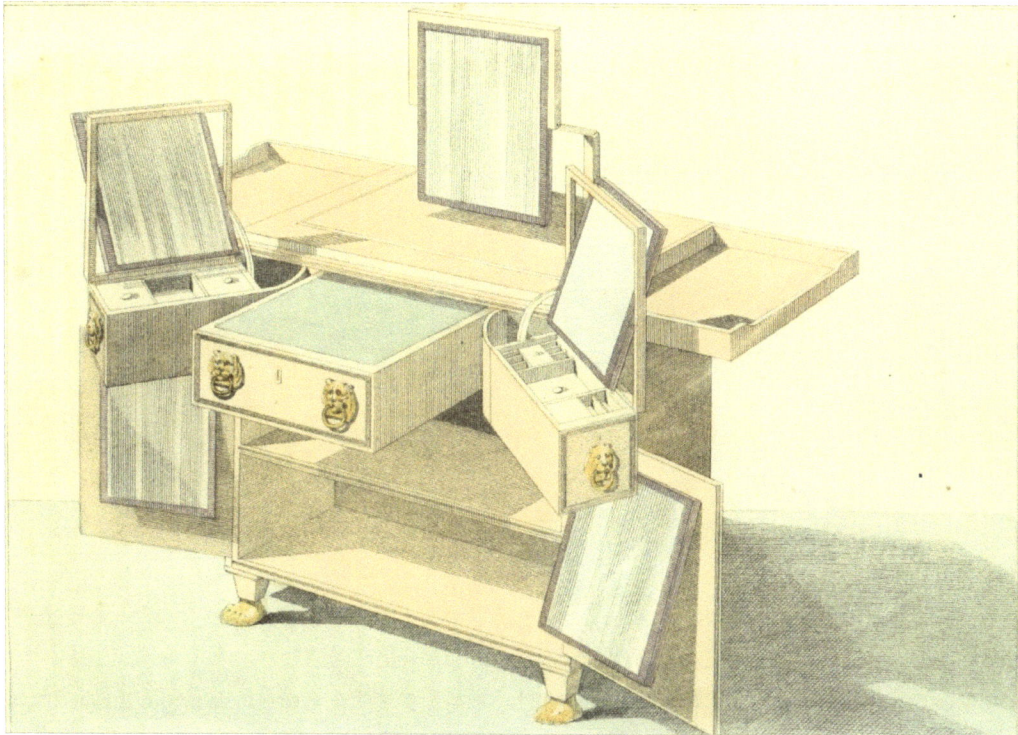

Ladies' Toilette Dressing-Case
April 1812

LADIES' TOILETTE DRESSING-CASE

The Ladies' toilette dressing-case, represented in our engraving, is the contrivance and workmanship of Messrs. Morgan and Sanders, whose ingenious labours in the production of interesting and ornamental furniture, we have so often the opportunity of submitting to the notice of our readers. The article represented in our engraving, exhibits, in a striking manner, the valuable combination of tasteful contrivance and arrangement, with excellent and beautiful workmanship. A dressing-case, with a folding opening lid or top, forms the body of the machine. At its front, and drawing out immediately from the under side of the top, is a sliding writing - drawer, or movable table, provided also with the usual requisites; and on either side of this, a small drawer, provided also with the usual arrangement of divisions, &c. for the reception of the articles used at the toilette: a large mirror rises from the back of the case, directly in front of the person seated at the table, and may be adjusted at pleasure, as to its height, distance, or angle. To each of the side drawers is also affixed, by joints, a mirror, adjustible at pleasure, as to its height, distance, or angle. To each of the side drawers is also affixed, by joints, a mirror, adjustible in the usual way, in its own frame, and by an ingenious contrivance of the drawer, movable also in the horizontal direction, enabling the lady herself to observe the profile, by reflection, in the front mirror, and the attendant to observe the front face, and the opposite profile by reflection, while herself is engaged on the nearer profile. The effect of the head, or whatever operation of the toilette is going on, may be judged of more quickly and accurately than is possible with the usual accommodation. On the inner sides of two folding doors, which inclose the lower part of the case, are suspended, on joints, two other mirrors, which are also adjustable in two directions, affording the same advantages with respect to the lower part of the figure.

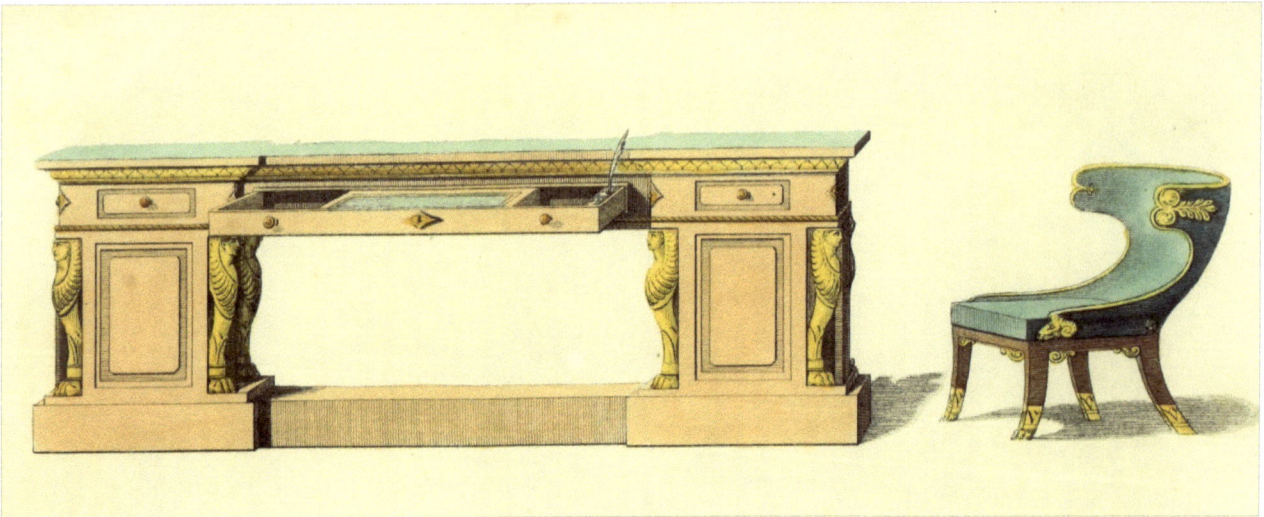

Library Table and Chair
May 1812

LIBRARY TABLE AND CHAIR

The library table and chair represented in our engraving for this month, are selected as two of the most appropriate articles now in use for the nobleman's and gentleman's library. The table forms a solid handsome piece of furniture, made to any scale in proportion to the room, with drawers, cupboards, a sliding writing-table in the center, ink, pens, &c.; handsomely ornamented with or-moulu brass-work and carved figures; the top covered with green morocco leather, and the chair en suite; the top yoke tastefully managed to guard and rest the head.

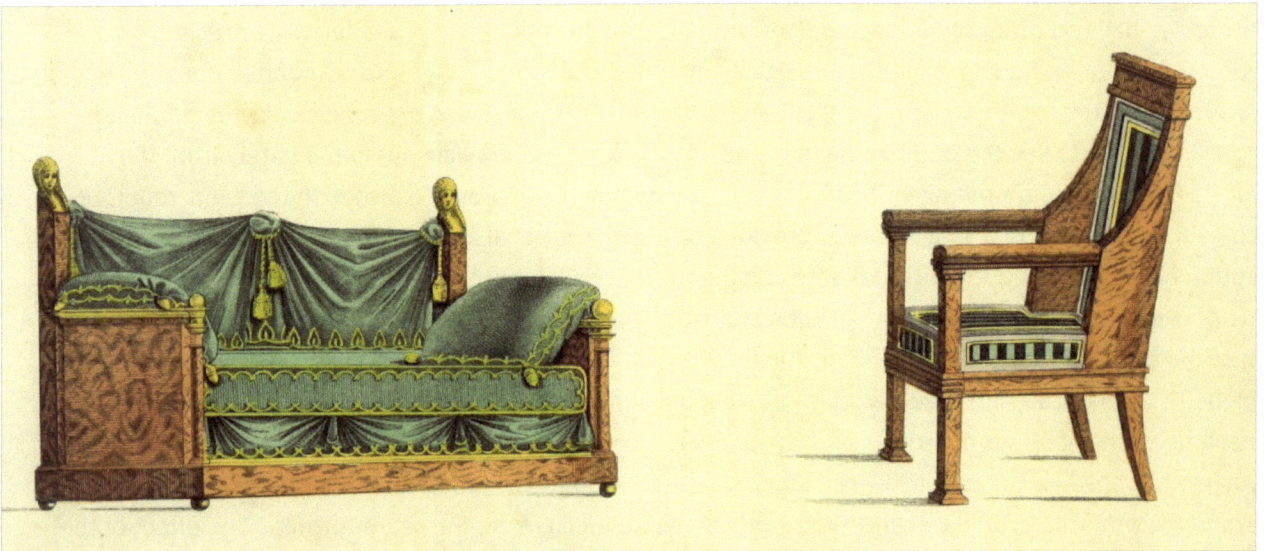

French Sofa and Drawing-Room Chair
June 1812

FRENCH SOFA AND DRAWING-ROOM CHAIR

The French sofa and drawing-room chair represented in the annexed engraving, are two articles well adapted for large mansions and castles, forming solid, comfortable, and handsome seats. The elevated backs of the sofa and chair, also, render them peculiarly pleasant and easy; the frames of both are of handsome mahogany, seats French stuffed, covered with silk, and handsomely ornamented with tassels, cord, &c.

39

French Curtain
July 1812

FRENCH CURTAIN

The French curtain represented in our engraving, has a simple, elegant drapery suspended on brass rosettes, ornamented with line and tassels. It is suited either for a library or morning room, in the cottage style; and may be made, to fancy, of any colour or kind of materials, suitable to the style and fitting up of the room, with mahogany dwarf book-cases, &c. &c. en suite.

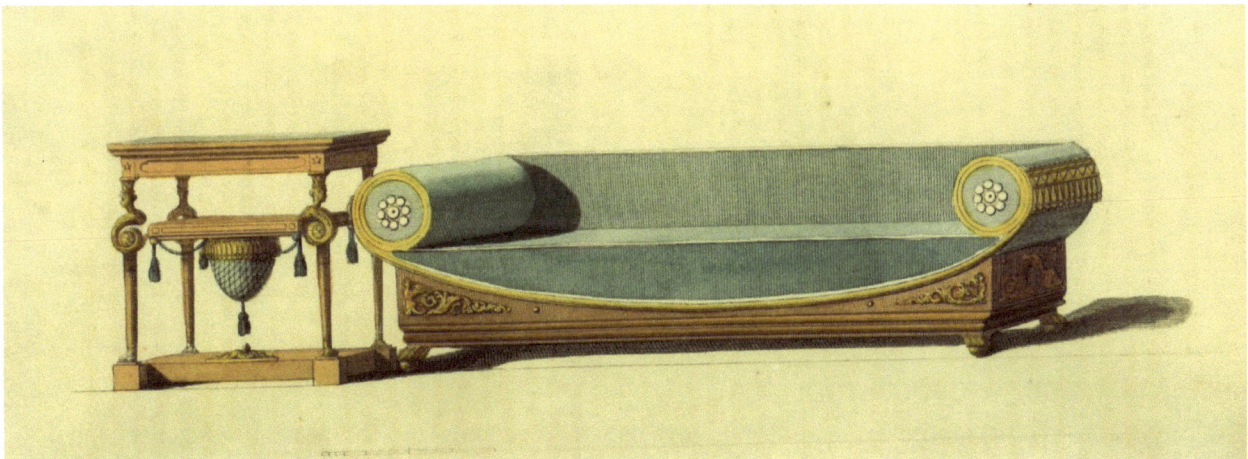

French Scroll Sofa
August 1812

FRENCH SCROLL SOFA

The annexed plate represents a beautiful French scroll sofa, adapted for the drawing-room, which may be made of rose- wood, with gold ornaments, and covered with rich chintz or silk tabouret, corresponding with the other parts of the furniture. It would also form a handsome sofa for the library, covered with Morocco leather, and the frame of mahogany richly ornamented with brass.

The accompanying French table forms an elegant lady's work-table, with silk bag, &c. en suite for the drawing- room.

Drawing-Room Window-Curtain
September 1812

DRAWING-ROOM WINDOW-CURTAIN

Our engraving this month represents an elegant drawing-room window-curtain, cornices, &c. complete, beautifully ornamented with French fringe, and extra muslin curtains, under the blue damask; a Grecian sofa and stool en suite, with a patent pedestal lamp; the whole of which are not less distinguished for their grandeur, than for simplicity and elegance.

Candelabrum, Table and Foot-Stool
November 1812

CANDELABRUM, TABLE AND FOOT-STOOL

The candelabrum represented in the annexed engraving, has been admired for its simple elegance, and is expressly designed in conformity to that general taste for uniting plainness with elegance, which prevails amongst the genteel class of the British public. The table partakes of the same character, simplicity of form, enriched, but not overloaded with ornament. This piece of furniture may be appropriated to many convenient purposes. It may be used with a portable desk for writing, for work, for the game of chess, or other amusing games that occupy but two persons. Neither of these specimens is of expensive execution.The foot-stool may afford a hint to those ladies who are desirous of exercising their taste on such elegant appendages to their sitting-room. A stool of this form, it is presumed, would appear handsome if covered with painted velvet.

Dwarf Book and Folio-Case
December 1812

DWARF BOOK AND FOLIO-CASE

The furniture plate for the present month exhibits a dwarf book and folio-case, suitable to a library or boudoir; it is replete with convenience for its intended purposes. The table -shelf, of dove marble, which separates the upper from the lower case, is of a width that will admit books and port-folios to rest upon for examination. The upper case is surmounted with a dove-marble shelf and bronze or or-moulu balustrum: in the center is a small gold-faced clock and drawer; on each side is a cabinet inclosure for books or papers: it is ornamented with four Persic pillars, and by masks of the Muses in bronze or or-moulu.

The lower case contains a range of drawers, a slide reading-shell, and three book-inclosures in front: at each end is a case for port-folios, with proper separations to keep them in an upright position, so essential to the preservation of prints and drawings. This part is decorated with masks of Hermes, wreaths and symbols of Genius and Study, and also with Persic pillars: the ornaments and handles are of bronze or of or-moulu.

The bookcase may be executed in mahogany, rose, or Coromandel wood, or indeed in any of the finer woods; and where a greater lightness of effect is desired, the pannel of the slides and doors may be covered with silk or drapery, to harmonize with the other furniture of the apartment.

Gothic Hall

The design for a Hall, of which the following observations are illustrative, is the first of a series purposed to be given in a few successive numbers of this publication. They are intended to display the decorations of some of the principal apartments of a mansion in the Gothic style. It is presumed, that they may be acceptable to the encouragers of the Repository of Arts, as affording' hints for works on an enlarged or a contracted scale; and not more on account of the general designs, than as they apply to the arrangement of the parts, and to the suitableness of the furniture.

These designs are submitted to the public with a hope, that they may in some degree further the progress of art; and they are presented with a full conviction, that this object is facilitated by all who demonstrate its principles and unveil its obscurities, since every art is most valued as it is best understood. As sculpture and painting are the handmaids of architecture, so are they immediately affected by all its diversities of state. In the decline or advancement of a country, architecture is the first to feel their influence, which is quickly imparted to its dependant branches. Indeed, the scions of art are so tenderly constituted, that they flourish only in the summer of a country's success, and are shrinkingly sensitive of the first blast that bespeaks the autumn of its glory.

The artist, in all ages, has, in his search after variety, rather preferred to adopt as models the works of former times, than dared to foster the offspring of his own imagination, although perhaps equally suited to the object, and no less consistent with the principles, of art and nature: thus, in our own time, the French style gave way to the Roman, that to the Greek; and as if the earlier ages must of necessity afford purer sources for research, the Persic and the Egyptian have been brought forward, and have failed to supersede those chaste models of harmony and truth that we yet contemplate with admiration, and imitate with respect.

The style of architecture called the Gothic, has fair claim to be considered as legitimate art, although so long rejected as an adventitious mixture of beauty and deformity. Probably the very term by which it has been known, has done much to injure its reputation, as we may have associated with it ideas of ignorance and barbarism. It is now almost rescued from these calumnies by the means that have been afforded for the cultivation of its beauties in the vast growth of foreign intercourse, riches, and leisure, which are the ostensible patrons of genius and taste. The greatness of outline, the delicacy of parts, the gracefulness of curvature, inexhaustible variety, and the contrasts of light and shade, in Gothic architecture, afford ample means for those beautiful combinations, which captivate and delight, and which will ever command a large portion of our highest estimation, by the fulness of its powers to interest and to controul the feelings of the human mind.

Modern improvement in the executive department, has greatly diminished the expence of structures in this style of art: the plastic apparatus has done much to supersede the chisel; and the advancement of geology and chemistry has, been attended by results in the composition of cements and artificial stones, that have formed an aera in the history of our architecture unexampled in other times. Advantage has been taken, in forming these designs, of the simple means thus afforded, and by which the burthen of expence would be avoided. These and other considerations, however, need not be dwelt upon, as the good sense of every person who builds, will intimate the propriety of consulting the ability, judgment, and taste, that distinguish the architects of the present day.

Speculations on the origin and progress of this style of art, do not necessarily form a part of these observations; it may not, however, be improper, to introduce a short sketch of its history.

After the Eastern and Western Empires had been overrun by the Goths and by the Saxons, Theodoric, King of the Ostrogoths, restored the city of Rome, and about the year 500, raised a considerable contribution for the purpose of completing this great object.

Of these buildings, however, which the Italians distinguished by the general term Tedeschi, or German, there exist no specimens correspondent in character with what is now called Gothic.

The Saxons, we may reasonably conclude, became impressed with the beauties of Grecian symmetry and contour, and endeavoured to ingraft some of those excellencies upon their own former style, rather than abandon it altogether: to this source, then, indicative as it must appear of intellectual darkness, and of the prejudices of education, we may ascribe that reversion and debasement of art so conspicuous in the architecture of the subsequent times.

Of that character of building termed Saxon, many vestiges yet remain; but so debased by a gradual decline of art through many ages, that at this time the vestiges of Grecian excellence scarcely admits of recognition. The columns, nevertheless, are round, have capitals and bases, and the arches are semicircles.

Out of this corrupted germ of Saxon art sprang that beautiful sublime imagery which we call Gothic; and although it may not be so amenable to rule, or so governed in its parts by laws of proportion hitherto understood, as the orders of the Greeks and Romans, it has, notwithstanding, been cultivated in an equal degree by men possessing the most brilliant fancy and soundest judgment.

However slow and uncertain the progress of this art may have been, the enlightened antiquary is enabled to mark the ages of its improvement, and frequently to develops its perfections.

The origin of the pointed arch, and the ornaments which decorate the Gothic structures, have afforded abundant opportunity for learned enquiry, and much hypothesis has been indulged upon these subjects.

Intersections of two or more Saxon arches, as frequently seen in buildings of this style, may easily be supposed to have suggested the pointed arch, on which great improvement may have been made by observations amidst groves of trees, which intermix their branches, not unlike to the windows and the vaultings of these edifices. Separated from Grecian models, the designers of these times appear to have sought principles of art in nature herself, and to have taken vegetation for their example. The principal lines, and those which indicate strength and support, are therefore always upright, and mark the peculiar character of Gothic architecture, in contradistinction to the Grecian and Roman, whose character is composed of horizontal lines.

The ornamental part has evidently been suggested by such plants as have been found in the neighborhood of these buildings, since they can be traced in most instances to the local plants; and these are generally disposed as in nature, where they trail along the ground, or cling to a fostering tree for protection: the neighborhood also supplied models for their statues.

It has been ingeniously observed, that the crescent tracery is of Saracenic origin, having been introduced on the return of the Crusaders from the Holy Wars. It is not, however, necessary to seek it in the eastern part of the globe, when it might have been found in the trefoil, the cinque foil, and the thistle at home. The riches afforded by the ample revenues of the church, aided by the studies of the enlightened monks, brought this art, by an irregular progress, to so high a degree of perfection towards the beginning of the sixteenth century, that it was said, in an exclamation of rapture, on beholding a building of the Gothic style — "This surely was knit together by the fingers of the angels!"

The sun dries up the barmy dews of the heavens, at the same time that it dispels the noxious vapours of the earth: so did the reformation of our national religion despoil and lay waste the architectural genius of the country, at the same time that it spread the light of reason, by dispelling the clouds of superstition. In revolutions so general and so extensive, every thing must give way; but it cannot be too severely lamented, that high talent at length joined issue with ignorance and folly: our great architects, Inigo Jones and Sir Christopher Wren, blended and associated with, the Gothic, the Roman and the Grecian orders of architecture; seemingly determined to avenge their debasement in the fourth and fifth centuries, by as completely debasing the Gothic in their own times.

The necessary limits of this publication do not admit the insertion of the observations that relate to the plate of the Gothic Hall. The number of next month will contain them in connection with those of the succeeding design; and as the subjects relate to each other, the descriptions will best appear together. (To be continued.)

Gothic Staircase and Vestibule

The censure bestowed upon Gothic architecture by professors of art, subsequent to the reformation of our national religion, and up to a very recent period, necessarily degraded it in the minds of those persons who had escaped the infection of early prejudices; and thus was continued a neglect of its beauties, long after the acknowledged influence of its charms. — Sir Christopher Wren, no less honoured on this account, for the sublime works which he produced in another style of art, mistook, or rather never understood, the principles of Gothic architecture; in the repairs of these edifices he appended designs in the Grecian style, and applied its peculiar principles to the restitution of Gothic structures, producing a false and incongruous arrangement, fatal to its beauties, and subversive of its powers to interest and delight: consequently, a censure was visited on the art itself, that belonged only to the architect, who never obtained an adequate understanding of its principles. Sir Christopher also seems to have decided and spoken of its merits, judging them by a standard not analogous to the object; for Gothic architecture merits distinction, as being perfectly independent, original, and generic.

That the art has suffered by these errors, is seriously to be lamented, because many beautiful parts of buildings have fallen into decay, and are no more. Our best acknowledgments are, however, due to a few men of taste, whose graphic records have preserved much; and we are greatly indebted to the gentlemen of the city and University of Oxford, whose liberal and enlightened minds have relieved the taste of our own times from such aspersions; and happily for science in future ages, their endeavours have been rendered effective by an architect whose penetrating research, discernment, and taste, enabled him to discover the principles of Gothic art, and to design new works with the truth of the originals, combined with all their genuine beauty.

Gothic architecture has erroneously been considered as unsuited to the purposes of domestic buildings, not from an actual experience of its unfitness, because we have no remains of such edifices by which to form conclusions, but because it is supposed to be of too grave, solemn, and gloomy a character: the reverse of this is the truth; and, upon investigating the beauties of the interior of Gothic structures, they will be found peculiarly light and elegant; it possesses a play of line, an intricacy of arrangement, and minuteness of parts, incapable of producing such impressions: it is the magnitude of these buildings, and an association of ideas, connecting with them ancient monastic austerities; it is the present devotional purposes to which they are applied, and the reverence we have for antiquity, that are the probable causes of this objection.

The architects in the twelfth, thirteenth, and fourteenth centuries, and indeed in earlier times, seem to have considered the forms and the arrangements of Gothic architecture, as deficient in solemnity of character, and therefore endeavoured to obtain the effect by other means: hence the excessive loftiness and space distinguishing Gothic cathedrals, seemingly magnified by a contrast of the ornamental parts; and hence the general adoption of coloured glass, producing a subdued and mysterious light,

> "Spreading sublimer gleams around,
> "Robed in the varied dyes of heaven."

The delicacy and elegance of the interior forms, so aided by quantity of space, by gloom, and by colour, must have been efficient to the object of the architect; but the latter means were not applicable to the outside of the building. It is evident, that he saw how unsuited the elegant designs of the interior were to produce a greatness and dignity of effect: he therefore used a massive character, perfectly associable, but not identified with them. The huge towers, the lofty spire, the ponderous and streight roof, were adopted;

Intentionally Left Blank

and the walls were encumbered by widely projecting buttresses; and if he decorated these by smaller parts, they were so arranged as not to deteriorate this effect, until, on a near approach, the building supplied all that the mind might lose of its seeming importance, by its real magnitude; and then, only, gave additional value to its majestic greatness, by obtaining respect, from its richness and its beauty.

The auxiliary plate is introduced for the purpose of showing, that the principle by which greatness of character is produced by Grecian architecture, is the reverse of that principle in the Gothic: the former commanding it by its important masses; the latter obtaining it by the quantity of air which it embraces. It is trusted, that these observations have proved, that Gothic architecture is capable of affording elegance to our mansions; and it is hoped, that the designs about to be spoken of, will be found to combine with it the means of domestic comfort and social enjoyment.

The Repository of the last month contained a design for a Gothic Hall; with this number is given an engraving of the Staircase and Vestibule. It will be perceived that they are not calculated for very large dimensions.

The hall is sufficiently spacious, and admits, by its form, which is a cross, four closets, appropriate to the use of the servants, and to receive coats, hats, sticks, &.c. The view is supposed to be taken from the entrance-door; the indication of the window will mark its scite, and the chimney-place is opposite: the floor is elevated by these steps about ten feet from the lower floor of the hall; a second staircase communicates to the vestibule, and leads to the chamber story; the principal apartments are also connected with the vestibule. It is essential to the interior arrangement of a residence, that the approach to the apartments should be direct and similar: if in the mind of the visitor they become confused, — if for one moment he is perplexed by its intricacies, it is fatal to those pleasurable sensations which all who build are desirous to create in the minds of their friends: a building only advances in the estimation of the spectator, as he is enabled to add room to room in a connected chain of association.

The hall should be of a character that will indicate a friendly hospitality: a contracted hall conveys an impression of meanness; if large and sumptuous, that of ostentation: regard should be therefore had to the judicious design, magnitude, and arrangement of the hall; for the earliest impression is generally the last to be effaced, and there is a climax in architecture as there is in oratory, and he would ill deserve the reputation of a Demosthenes or a Cicero, whose first sentence was so elevated and emphatic as to render flat and insipid those parts of his address which required to be eminently dignified and impressive. The hall is so designed as to admit an increased feeling of respect.

The ceiling, although vaulted, is of a horizontal character. This room is not over lighted, and of a simple design. At the steps commences the apparent occupancy of the superior; the oak screen and enriched candelabra bespeak it; the corridor, right and left, gives the idea of extent to the building; ascending the stairs, from the horizontal to the highly elegant vertical archway and vestibule, the mind becomes prepared for those Impressions which the apartments should be equal to produce, and which should result us much from contrast and combination, as from own intrinsic excellence. It will be perceived that the designs become more decorated as they proceed; the arrangement of the ornaments, the design of the furniture, and the harmony of the consistency.

Gothic Conservatory

51

Among the means adopted for the purposes of elegant and useful recreation, the Conservatory is pre-eminent; in few instances has it been cultivated to an extent that might be expected in our climate, which, by its variableness and sudden transitions, gives increased importance to such resources as may be afforded by our homes. When the weather is unfavourable, the Conservatory presents a promenade, where the advantages of exercise and air may be obtained, and where the eye will be delighted with the beauty of the plants, and the ear by the melody of the aviary, which is a most desirable addition; the fragrance of the flowers will add to these charms, and an endless interest will be afforded to the mind of taste, and to the botanist, who will find in the Conservatory an admirable substitute for more lengthened excursions. If health, the offspring of exercise; if the welfare of the mind, certainly very intimately connected with rational and pleasurable impressions, be worth our serious regard, surely this means, which at all seasons so well affords them, merits the highest cultivation: in winter it is a warm, and in summer a cool retreat from the severities of each, and many hours in both have been applied with additional delight to books in these retirements, which is ever suited to recreation and to study. The Gothic style admits a construction of building so light and elegant, that it adds charms to those of nature, combined with which, in this instance, it would seem to realize those dreams of fancy, in which we sportively paint to our imaginations the palaces of the sylphs and genii.

The design which accompanies these observations, is constructed on one of many forms that would be applicable to the purposes of a Conservatory: it is of a round figure, and thereby admits a circular promenade; a reservoir of water is in the center, and might contain gold and silver fish. The entrance to the vestibule is at the steps in front, a bath is opposite to this; and on each side are rooms, forming aviaries.

Notwithstanding the simplicity of this figure, a very great variety of effect would be produced. The motion of the spectator would seem to be transferred to the surrounding subjects, and at every step the disposition of them must appear to change; the jet d'eau would unite in producing this object with the plants and with the pillars, and an effect consequently be obtained perfectly unique and fascinating.

The groined dome in the center, which is supported by the surrounding pillars, would be of tracery, filled up with glass, so that the sky and the clouds might be conspicuous through it. This would produce a very beautiful effect in a bright evening, when the spangled canopy of the heavens would assist in the decoration. The dome is so elevated, that the rays of the sun could not be too obtrusive; the windows of the lower parts would open to the ground and to the shrubberies, in the manner of folding sashes, and they are of coloured glass. In the design, transparent blinds are introduced, but of one general colour, for occasional purposes: as, to exclude the sun; for the evening, when the Conservatory might be lighted up; or in winter, to produce an effect of warmth. The pedestals between the pillars might contain sculptured ornaments, or such articles of variety or elegance as would interest by their merits, and add richness by their forms and colour; if such things are selected and arranged with taste, they never fail to please.

Gothic Bedchamber and State Bed

In France it is now considered to be essential, that the architect should design the furniture, as well as the building executed under his direction, as unity of character is highly valued, which cannot be obtained, unless the whole is guided by the same mind. To a very different practice this country is indebted for the ill effects of our buildings, furnished as they are, under as many different feelings of taste as there may be articles of furniture: sometimes, indeed, it happens that the architect's aid does not cease quite so soon, and the advantage is always discernible in the proportions and the fitness of the parts to the whole, and to each other, which in the language of art, is called composition. If in a picture this be neglected, it is not compensated for even by the hues of Titian, or the drawing of Michael Angelo. How, then, may we hope that the interior of our buildings will obtain admiration and respect, when the architect is consulted no farther than the surfaces of the design, and the completion is entrusted to the painter, the decorator, the upholsterer, draper, carpet - maker, mason, smith, in their various departments. For, notwithstanding each may be eminent in his respective line, an incongruous association is the inevitable result, and those unarchitectural monstrosities are produced, which have lately disgraced ingenuity and taste.

The design of a Gothic chamber is intended to display its form, its decoration, and its furniture. The walls are divided into compartments by mullions and tracery. The hangings are of blue silk; and the ornaments, velvet, of a darker colour. The bed is formed on the principle of the Gothic crosses of Queen Eleanor, and of a wood corresponding with yellow or orange wood of the mullions: portions of this are gilded. From the pinnacles rise groined arches, to support a Gothic canopy, from which are suspended the hangings of the bed, of a tent-like character. The base of the bedstead extends on each side, where steps are made to rise, as the steps to a throne, and they are continued, from the head to the foot, the whole length of the bed; and, for convenience, they may be made occasionally to slide under it. The hangings are of orange silk, lined with blue, and with blue ropes and tassels. This silk might be of those rich patterns which are found painted as the draperies of Gothic statues. If the hangings of the room, the bed, and the curtains were of this character, an unusually rich and splendid effect would be produced. The cabinets and sofas should be finished to correspond with the other furniture. The carpet is designed to suit the form of the room, and the arrangement of the furniture; it is of a Gothic figure, and the colours are intended to harmonize with them.

In furnishing a room, we cannot be too solicitous respecting the arrangement of the forms, the propriety of character, the due proportion of the vertical to the horizontal lines, in fact, to the composition of the whole: for it is not simply that a handsome bed, or sofa, or cabinet, or grate is suited to a handsome room; for if each does not, by the principles of composition, correspond with the other parts they tend to destroy the harmony, and are fatal to the elegance and the pleasurable end of our endeavours .

The blue and cool colour is here introduced to give effect to the orange, which is a warm one; and the furniture of the bed is of the latter colour, that its richness and quantity may operate as the light of a picture, to lead the attention to that which is the most important feature of the subject and the composition.

Gothic Book-Room

The room of business, the justice-room, or that appropriated to pamphlets, records, and those papers not immediately the proper furniture of the library, forms the subject of the design which accompanies this description. Its situation should not be far removed from the principal hall, and in the vicinity of a private entrance, which admits of approach without passing through the hall or the servants' apartments, for the convenience and the introduction of tenants and other persons on mere business. It is the legitimate apartment of the secretary, in establishments of a magnitude to entertain them, or it is the superior room for the purposes of the steward and the transaction of the business of the estate.

A chaste and simple character is best suited to these objects: the plate, which presents a geometrical view of the chimney-piece side of this room, is intended to give an appropriate design, and of a degree of solidity, and consequently seeming strength, which may accord with the uses of the apartment. The arches divide the room into three portions, and give an architectural arrangement of the furniture very desirable; it affords an elevation, a variety, and an intricacy to the design of the ceiling, and produces a stateliness of effect.

The cases, the repositories of the papers and records, are formed of polished oak, and of such a design as to add the appearance of greater magnitude to the study. The chimney-piece, which forms a part of the design of the cases, is made of marble, the verd antique, the Sienna, or our native marbles, some of which are of uncommon brilliance, and are to be found in ample quantities for such purposes. Lord Gwydir has greatly encouraged the introduction of them. Sufficient for purposes was lately selected at Portsoy, in Scotland, by Sir David Wedderburn, Bart. And was sculptured in London, for the principal chimney-pieces and bookcases of his lately erected residence in Essex; and proves to be of great excellence and beauty .

Indeed our native marbles are deserving public cultivation, and many of them approach to the perfection of the antiques. With much plausibility, though not with evidence amounting to conviction, the late Sir George Wright maintained, that the verd antique was of British origin, having opened a long neglected quarry in Wales, which affords marbles of similar appearance, and corresponding in the analysis. As the country where this precious marble was produced, is not known by the virtuosi of the present day, he deemed this a tacit corroboration of his hypothesis. When we see men of rank and fortune interesting themselves in the adoption of marbles, the produce of their native country, we have cause to hope that they will obtain an universal interest and patronage.

The shelf of the chimney-piece is continued through the bookcase, and forms a sort of table-shelf in front of them, for the reception of books and papers: the plinth of cases.

The application of oak to the Gothic style of architecture, has always been considered as affording great beauty, both by colour and by contrast. The Gothic screens and wainscotings, the railing and canopies of our cathedrals, present many fine examples of design and workmanship in this material: indeed, there is something so English both in the design of Gothic edifices and in the oaken embellishments which accompany them, that we are impressed by an interest in structures of this kind intimately connected with national feelings.

Gothic Library

June 1813 - Gothic Book-Room (continued)

The manufacture of oak into furniture and other articles of taste and usefulness, has undergone an extraordinary improvement in point of workmanship, and it is now wrought with so much elegance as to rival the more expensive woods of other countries. The vast improvement also in taste, and the art of design and sculpture of the human figure, has given an excellence to modern works unknown to the ages of Gothic art. The figures sculptured in wood on the pediment of the altar-piece of the church of St. Paul's, Covent-Garden, are not generally known, but are of great merit: the simple elegance of the interior of that church, fitted up entirely of oak, deserves much approbation. It is not, however, in the Gothic style, which would have been unsuited to the original design by Inigo Jones, whose instruction for the plan received from an ancestor of the Bedford family, was, to make it "as spacious and as simple as a barn." Jones therefore chose the Tuscan order as given by Vitruvies; not that he preferred a barn-like character, whatever he might have done had he lived to see the principle generally pursued by men of no taste, who have saved themselves the labour in indeed, but have lost the delight of architectural fitness, by substituting overwhelming draperies of meretricious forms and colours, in lieu of the elegant, chaste, and Grecian, Roman, or Gothic styles.

It is intended that the design of the following month shall be a perspective view of a room formed on a similar plan, but treated as a Library, with the books exposed, and the apartment furnished applicably to its purpose.

July 1813 - Gothic Library

The observations contained in the Repository of last month, are applicable to the present design, which represents a library of a more elevated and richer character, on a similar ground plan.

This view exhibits the window, side, and the end of the room, and more fully displays the effect of the arches and the diversity of form, of light, and of shadow. The windows, which may be of stained glass, form a bay of considerable magnitude, in which the sofas and the reading-table may be placed. This spot would become a very cheerful portion of the room, and derive an effect of superior brilliance, by a contrast with the more retired parts, which would be lighted only by the rays passing from this opening, and variously subdued by refraction and by colour. A chimney-glass should be opposite to the opening, which would reflect the objects contained in the bay, and also the coloured windows and landscape beyond them.

In the corners of the center compartment are disposed marble altars and bronze candelabra. On the pedestals of the cases are ranged the busts of persons who have been eminent in science, arts, or literature; a tribute of respect to them, merited by their labours of study and research, and by an endeavour to render their attainments beneficial to mankind; a tribute useful to ourselves, as it encourages the advancement of moral intellect, and the fulfilment of those great purposes for which it is subjected to our government.

Recesses are formed in the pedestal to receive the seats, which, by tins arrangement, leave the area of the apartment free and unincumbered, and add a more splendid effect to the eases themselves.

The very high perfection to which the art of book-binding has arrived, and the fashion for adopting such embellishments, has given great importance to the library, which has become a room of usual resort, and also forms an object of female cultivation in no less degree than the drawing-room. The fascinations of female society have added taste to the energies of study, and have blended the gracefulness of polished life with the severer attainments of learning; the gloom of seclusion is banished from its walls, and its means are aided by the charms of beauty

"To raise the genius, and to mend the heart."

In the present design is contained a contrivance to secure the books from injury, which is easily applied, and adds to the decoration: the plate is, however, too small to admit of a graphic illustration. It is a drapery of silk, suspended within side and at the top of the case, by a spring roller, in the manner of a blind, and is made to draw to the bottom of the case, where spring-locks are placed to receive the means for confining it; they are connected at the side by grooves, and thus become as protecting as doors would be, without their weight or inconvenience.

END OF SERIES
A Mansion in the Gothic Style

Dwarf Table and Cabinet
February 1813

DWARF TABLE AND CABINET

A perfectly new and very useful piece of furniture is contained in the plate of the present month: it is a dwarf table, suitable to the library, sitting-room, or boudoir. Its application is to hold books, or the articles of study and amusement, in aid of the secretary or work-table, and is placed on the right of the person so engaged. At other times, it affords an elegant support for vases of flowers, and other useful or ornamental purposes. The top is of marble, and the frame is decorated with or-molu and ebony.

The remaining portion of the plate represents a design for a cabinet. It may be formed of mahogany, satin-wood, or rose- wood, inlaid with brass and ebony: the embossed ornaments are in or-molu.

The interior may be fitted up with shelves, drawers, or in compartments, suitable to the medalist and the antiquary.

Pocock's Reclining Chair
March 1813

POCOCK'S RECLINING CHAIR

   Our engraving this month represents an elegant fashionable fauteuil chair, upon Messrs. Pocock's patent reclining principle, to incline the back to any position, with double reclining footstools, which slide from under the chair to extend it when the back is reclined to the length of a couch. A reading-desk is attached to the side, and contrived to swing round in front of the chair. The whole is designed with classical taste, in the present improved fashion of modern furniture, by the ingenious inventors, Messrs. Pocock's, of Southampton-street, Covent- Garden.

State Bed
May 1813

STATE BED

This extremely neat and elegant bed furnishes us with a handsome specimen of what our intelligent and ingenious upholsterers may effect in articles of plain furniture, when they are designed with taste, and executed with some regard to the symmetry and effect of the tout-ensemble.

This piece of furniture is a plain patent mahogany framed bed, with elevated cornices, in a military style, and of suitable and appropriate ornamental workmanship: their curved figure, with the bolder sweeps of the draperies which are disposed on them, gives an air of loftiness and consequence, without appearing too massive, and preserves a desirable airiness of style. The canopy top, with the surmounting ornaments, also adds considerably to the effect, when the height of the apartment admits of it. The radiating head-cloth is produced by plaiting, and has in the furniture a very simple and pleasing appearance.

The drawing of this subject is made by C. Blunt, from Messrs. Morgan and Saunders's Rooms; Catharine-street, Strand.

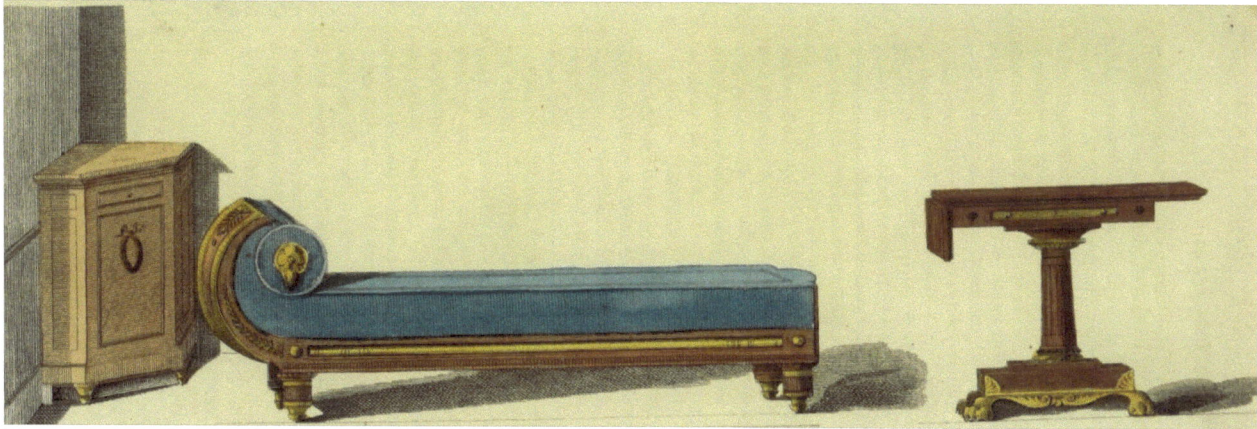

Antique Sofa and Table
August 1813

ANTIQUE SOFA AND TABLE

The antique sofa and table presented in the annexed plate, are designed as accompaniments to other, and are therefore imagine upon similar principles of taste. It is not sufficient, that the ornaments and the colours of the furniture should correspond, but a harmony of this principle must pervade the whole; without which, our endeavours to obtain the requisites of the agreeable, the elegant, or the beautiful in furniture, will be defeated. To illustrate this position, too little regarded in the art of design in the furnishing department, a third piece is represented, ornamental in itself, but obviously constructed with other feelings of style, and it thence becomes incongruous with the table and the sofa: in these the quantity of horizontal and of vertical lines are similarly proportioned, but in the former piece (an angle pedestal) this proportion is destroyed, and the upright lines, predominate, without so complete a transition as would render it the means of connecting the furniture with the architectural embellishments of the apartment: candelabra and tripods admirably effect this object, and, from their decided character, do not militate against the effect of either.

The sofa and the table may be executed of satin, Coromandel, or rose wood, of ebony or of mahogany, decorated with bronze, or-molu, or with carvings in the respective or contrasting woods.

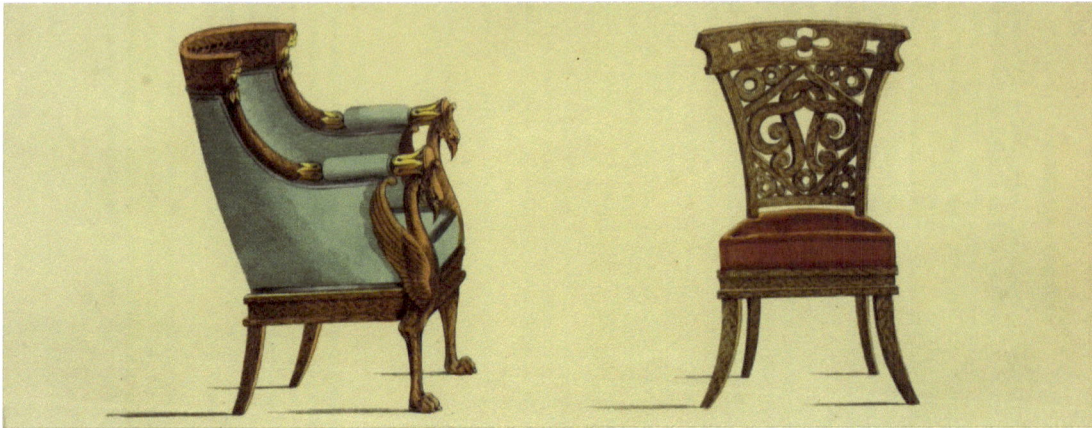

Bed-Room and Cottage Chair
September 1813

BED-ROOM AND COTTAGE CHAIR

The bed-room chair is of the highest character of decoration, and of course adapted to the principal chambers of a mansion: the frame is of mahogany, of satin wood, or may be painted in imitation of them. The form of this chair is suited for repose.

The cottage chair is composed after the designs which prevailed in the sixteenth century, when the national taste was yet unsettled, and the fancy adopted forms and embellishments not in unison with the refined and classic taste of modern times: the very circumstance, probably, makes this design analogous to the purposes of a cottage ornée; and it has lately been introduced with great advantage as furniture for buildings of the castellated character, and also for those whose original features are of similar construction, and to which furniture has been introduced much less in harmony, although, separately considered, of a superior design.

The plate (No. 4,) given in the Repository for July, is a French window-curtain: it is designed for a room where the space between the windows is of excessive dimensions, which very frequently occurs in old buildings. To relieve this defect, and also to remove the objectionable appearance of a central pier, a mirror is substituted for an opening, and the effect of three distinct spaces is produced by the architectural embellishments: circular cornices, in the manner of the archivolts of the Romans, are supported by therms, and from these arches are suspended the curtains, which accompany the pier glass in the center also. The tablet is introduced in the usual manner. The flower-stands, on the extremes of the design, are suited to the dining and the drawing-rooms.

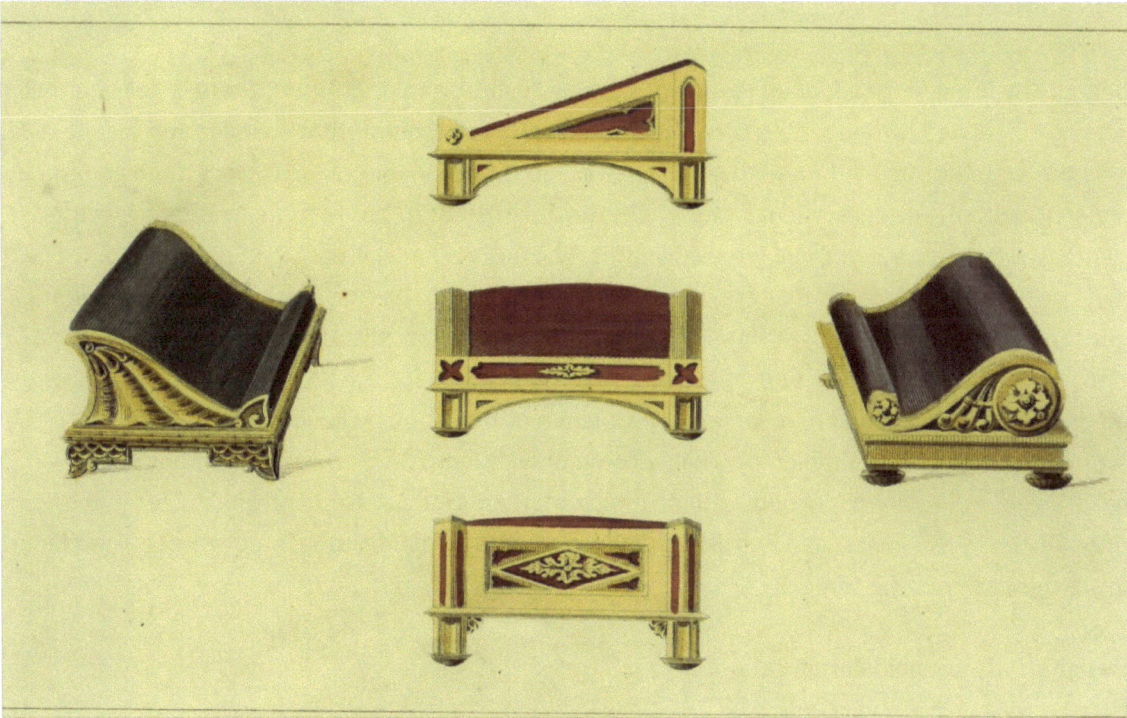

Footstools
October 1813

FOOTSTOOLS

Of the various secondary trades and professions, few have availed themselves more of the specimens brought forward to improve our national taste, than the manufacturers of household furniture; notwithstanding it was stated a few years since, in a noted publication , that there was not then to be found "one professional man at once possessed with sufficient intimacy with the stores of literature, to suggest ideas, and of sufficient practice in the art of drawing, to execute designs, that might be capable of ennobling, through means of their shape and their accessories, things so humble in their chief purpose and destination as a table and a chair, a footstool and a screen." — The young artist who might endeavour to remove that deficiency, was there also cautioned, not to confine his exertions to a servile copying of what has been done, nor continue in that track, which could only make him move, as heretofore, in an eternal round of undeviating sameness; but to ascend to those higher, those more copious sources of elegance, those productions of Nature herself, animate and inanimate, which contain the first elements and the first models of all the perfections of art; not omitting those monuments of antiquity in which the forms of nature are most happily adapted, and which, when united, can alone offer an inexhaustible store of ever varied and ever novel beauties.

But how, we will ask, is so great a change in household furniture to be effected? Can we expect the artizans and manufacturers to alter their present mode of education, and ascend to the study of those higher and more copious sources of elegance ? or are our artists and architects to descend, in making it their business to point out and correct the designs suitable for carpets, or the manner of making up window-curtains, articles which will be ever used and adopted in these more northern climates ? — When that takes place, then alone can we expect to find our furniture in unison with our mansions, and the whole in a style truly classical. But in this we beg leave to be understood, as making general observations only, justified and founded on the knowledge of many bright exceptions in both departments.

FOOTSTOOLS (Continued)

It has been justly remarked, that of all the various articles in household furniture, there is not one that has been so neglected, and carried with it that sameness through all the different changes and recent styles of fashion, as the footstool; and yet none that has been in more fashionable request, or in more general use.

The Grecian footstool, an engraving of which we here-with present to our readers, was first executed from a design furnished by Mr. Gregson, whose scientific abilities we have already had occasion to notice.

This article possesses advantages that are not immediately seen on the first inspection, independent of the chasteness of design: the angle of inclination given to the surface, receives the foot in its natural and most easy position; while the smaller part of the scroll serves as a stay for the heel, and prevents the whole from being- propelled forward; and in reversing the situation of the stool, by having the smaller scroll from you, it answers the purpose of a jambier, or what is commonly called a comfort and ease. They have been finished, for drawing-rooms, in rose-wood, with or-molu ornaments, and carved and gilt trusses and feet; also in bronze and gold, and in mat and burnished gold, covered with plain and painted velvets. The Chinese and Gothic are designs after the same plan.

---

* Hope's Designs for Household Furniture, p. 7.

Library Table and Chair
January 1814

LIBRARY TABLE AND CHAIR

The chaste and elegant library table, represented in the annexed engraving, is of a convenient form and moderate size, and is suited to an apartment of small dimensions: at the same time it exhibits that breadth of parts and greatness of design, which characterize most ornaments of bronze; the shelves articles of modern furniture, and give a dignity heretofore unknown. The recess beneath renders it also extremely commodious for a writing-table, which was not the case with the library tables formerly constructed. The chair is designed with equal attention to elegance and convenience, and made to correspond. They may both be formed of mahogany, with rings and ornaments of bronze; the shelves of the table will divide, so as to admit either a row of folios and octavos, or two rows of quartos.

riting and Backgammon Table
February 1814

WRITING AND BACKGAMMON TABLE

The very elegant and tasteful article represented in the annexed engraving, is intended to serve the double purpose of usefulness and pleasure. In the first, it is convenient as a breakfast or as a sofa table; it also forms a convenient writing or drawing-table, with drawers for paper, colours, pencil, &c. For the second, a sliding board for the games of chess, drafts, backgammon, &c. which slides under the desk. It is very light, goes upon castors, and is particularly pleasant to sit before, as there is sufficient accommodation for the knees by its projecting top.

The chair is contrived for study or repose. Its sweeping form is calculated to afford rest to the invalid; and the arms are sufficiently low to allow it to be used at the writing or reading-desk. It is lighter than its form would indicate, and it is easily moved, being placed upon traversing castors.

Lady's Book-Case
March 1813

LADY'S BOOK-CASE

This elegant and novel piece of furniture is calculated for a lady's boudoir, being extremely light, and occupying but a very small space. It is contrived to serve as an escrutoire and repository for various articles, which may be inclosed within the folding doors beneath the drawers. The gilt ornaments upon each door, relieved upon the silk curtains, produce a pleasing and tasteful effect; and when the whole is closed, it has the appearance of an elegant cabinet.

The book-case from which this design was made, is manufactured by Messrs. Morgan and Sanders, Catherine-street, Strand.

Carlton House Table and Chair
April 1814

CARLTON HOUSE TABLE AND CHAIR

We know that a people become enlightened by the cultivation of the arts, and that they become great in the progress of that cultivation. That a just knowledge of the useful and a correct taste for the ornamental so hand in hand with this general improvement, the dullest observer may be satisfied by looking around him.

We now acknowledge, that it is alone the pencil of the artist which can trace the universal hieroglyphic; understood alike by all, his enthusiasm communicates itself to all alike, and prepares the mind for cultivation. A national improvement is thus produced by the arts, and the arts are supported in their respectability by the calls which the improving public taste makes tor their assistance; they are inseparable in their progress, and mutually depend on each other for support. In the construction of the domestic furniture of our dwellings we see and feel the benefit of all this. To the credit of our higher classes who encourage, and of our manufacturing artists who produce, we now universally quit the overcharged magnificence of former ages, and seek the purer models of simplicity and tasteful ornament in every article of daily call.

The table and chair which are the subject of the present engraving, are peculiarly of the description of improvement of which we are speaking. They exhibit a judicious combination of elegance and usefulness, do great credit to the artists who designed and executed them, and highly merit the patronage afforded them.

They are from the ware-rooms of Messrs. Morgan and Sanders, of Catherine-street, Strand. They take the name of Carlton-House Table and Chair, as we presume, from having been first made for the august personage whose correct taste has so classically embellished that beautiful palace.

Drapery Window-Curtains
May 1814

DRAPERY WINDOW-CURTAINS

Among the variety of advantages derived from the fine arts, perhaps the most prominent is, the faculty of commemorating passing events. The efforts of the pencil produce indelible impressions on the mind. Painting is to the eye what poetry is to the ear. An event related in harmonious verse warms the imagination and acquires additional interest; but the painter collects in his design scattered and collateral occurrences, the eye comprehends at one view- each particular circumstance, and the mind, wrapt up in the object before it, suffers no distraction: we are insensibly transported amid the group delineated on the canvas; we cease to be mere spectators, we actually participate for the moment in the scene before us. — The memory being more strongly impressed with what we see, than with that which is only a subject of narration, produces this superiority of painting over the sister art. The sight of an object possessing any allusion to a past event, seldom fails to excite all those feelings of which the circumstance itself was capable. The wish to obtain this gratification is natural and honourable, and he who exercises his talent in the promotion of this feeling, promotes the best interests of society.

We generally delight to cherish the recollection of a memorable event by reference to surrounding objects. In a minor class of productions of this nature, our domestic furniture is well calculated to produce this effect, when so contrived as to be sufficiently conspicuous, without being obtrusive. Many articles of furniture have lately been offered to the public, which combine purity of invention with much elegance and utility: for this we are indebted to the

Improved taste of the age, which sees the necessity of inviting the professional ability of the artist in the appropriate arrangement of domiciliary decoration. The manufacturer finds it necessary to anticipate the wants of his employer, and to call for the assistance or the arts, to furnish him with such designs as the season and circumstances may require: this frequent application to professional talent for correct design, induces artists of the higher order to bend themselves to it, and submit the luxuriant production of their imaginations to the practical experience of the manufacturing tradesman. Tins is highly creditable to both parties; it marks the taste of the latter, and the desire of the former to render his pencil more diffusively useful. But we must refer all this to its real source — the munificent encouragement afforded by the higher classes.

The late glorious events which have so thickly crowded on us, give a new spur to such exertions. Tin design for a suit of drapery window-curtains, represented in our present plate, is produced under the inspection of Morgan and Sanders, of Catherine-street, Strand, who so constantly distinguish themselves as indefatigable caterers for the public taste. The whole design and colouring of the drapery are correct and appropriate. The azure and white, which may he sprinkled with lilies, are the colours of the legitimate dynasty of France, and are beautifully correspondent with the opening season. The eagle of Russia surmounts the whole, in allusion both to the superiority she has obtained in arms, and in just compliment to her magnanimous forbearance, and her noble and respectful conduct towards the French capital, as a seat of the fine arts. The doves sporting with laurel, the insignia of victory, are emblematical of confidence, and of the security and repose of peace, to whom the ensigns of war are no longer terrible. Indeed to the fertile imagination, this design, though not incumbered with ornament, will appear replete with the most delicate conceits and comprehensive allusions; and will probably lay the ground-work of happier efforts in emblematical and splendid furniture, than have yet been produced.

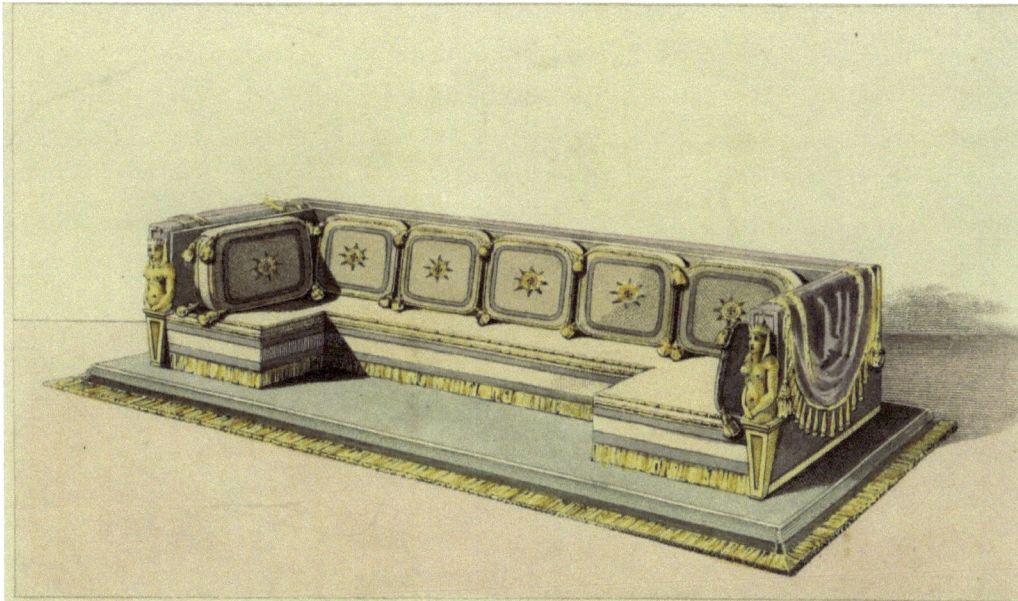

Ottoman Couch
July 1814

OTTOMAN COUCH

The present plate of splendid furniture is the design of an artist for an Ottoman couch or sofa. — This article, although susceptible of great diversity of form and arrangement, and an unbounded variety of decoration, is yet so simple in its general figure, and so easily understood in all its parts, from a judicious drawing, that our present plate requires no explanation.

We may here, however; be allowed to repeat, what we have already so frequently alluded to, that taste in matters of decoration, in whatever node of application, or to whatever subject, is only to be acquired by, or expected from, that general and miscellaneous knowledge, which it is the avowed and constant object of our publication to recommend and promote. Our manufactures must now have, not merely that strength of fabric and that durability of texture, in which once consisted their highest praise; but they are required to possess elegance of design, novelty of pattern, and beauty of finishing: to effect these, all the aid of improved and refined art is essentially necessary.

Bed Chamber Chairs
August 1814

BED CHAMBERS CHAIRS

The annexed plate exhibits three designs for light chairs intended for bed-chambers, for secondary drawing-rooms, and occasionally to serve for routs. These chairs may be stained black, or, as the present taste is, veined with vitriol, stained with logwood, and polished to imitate rose-wood; the seats caned.

No. 1. should he japanned, to imitate bamboo. The ornaments on the yoke and other parts black.

No. 2. may be black or rose-wood colour; the ornamental parts metal or gilt. The circular ornament on the yoke should be cut through the edges, moulded, and gilt.

No. 3. is proposed to be finished in a similar style; the balls metal: the splats in the back are cut through at their base, to give lightness to their effect. — These patterns, as drawn, are not meant to have cushions.

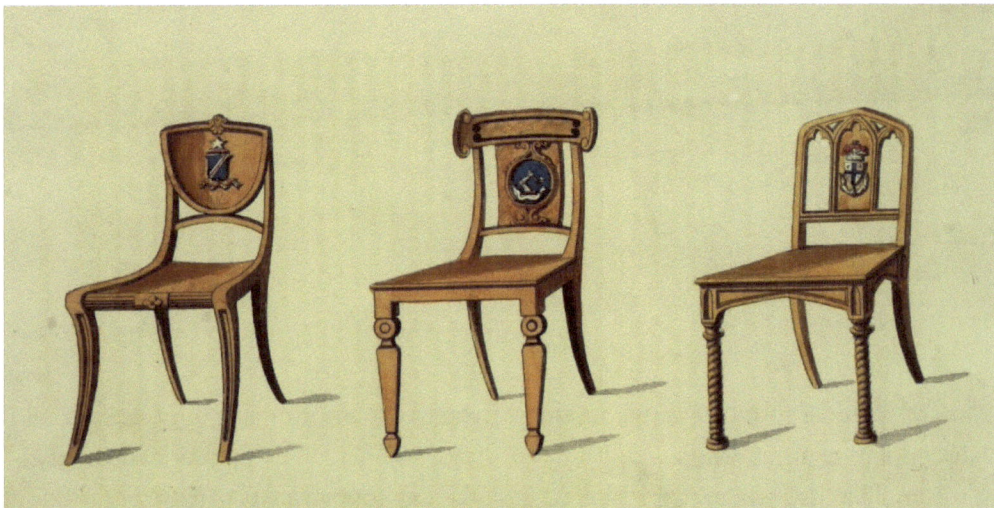

Hall Chairs
September 1814

HALL CHAIRS

Nos. 1. and 2. are chairs for halls of solid mahogany, the ornamental parts carved in the same wood; the pannels in the front legs sunk out of the solid wood. In No. 2. the parts in black are of ebony: the finishing, in other respects, as No.1.

No. 3. a chair in the Gothic taste, adapted for cottages or Gothic mansions. It is here intended to be of oak; the Gothic relievo carved, or it may be painted in imitation of the same wood, and relieved by shadows, to have a good effect.

Parlour Chairs
October 1814

PARLOUR CHAIRS

No. 1. A dining-room chair of mahogany, the ornamental parts on the splat or yoke being of bronzed metal; the seat of cane, and the cushion, separate, secured by straps underneath.

No. 2. A chair of Grecian form, the whole of mahogany, except the ornament on the knees of the front legs, which are of bronzed metal; the back and feet are loose, and stuffed on frames made to screw in.

No. 3. A Grecian parlour chair, otherwise called Trafalgar, after the late Lord Nelson; the yoke inlaid; with ebony; the ornamental parts in bronzed metal; and the wreath and patera in the back are laid on a solid mahogany ground. This seat is loose, stuffed on a frame, secured in its place with screws under the rails.

Drawing-Room Chairs
December 1814

DRAWING-ROOM CHAIRS

No 1 is supposed to be made of rose-wood, the ornamental parts, with the fillets, to be finished in gold. The seat is stuffed in a loose frame, and made to fit exactly to its place when covered and finished. The stuffed back is also a loose frame, screwed in from the back of the chair.

No. 2. A chair for similar rooms, in black, and the ornamental parts gold. This chair has a cushion made to fit exactly to the seat which is either caned or covered with strong linen.

Library Window-Curtain
January 1815

LIBRARY WINDOW-CURTAIN

It is a common defect in building, attributable to the tax upon windows, that a sufficient number of them are not introduced for the purposes of cheerfulness; and there are many rooms lighted by so few, and the dimensions of them so small, that not only an insufficient supply of light is admitted, but the windows are too narrow, and their dressings too circumscribed to form proportions suited to the apartments. The annexed plate represents a window of this kind, with the added architectural finishings, by which it is so increased as to have the proportion of a Palladian or Venetian one, and a design for a curtain suitable to it is introduced in a style adapted to a library or eating-room. It is a design very applicable to some rooms which have but one window in each.

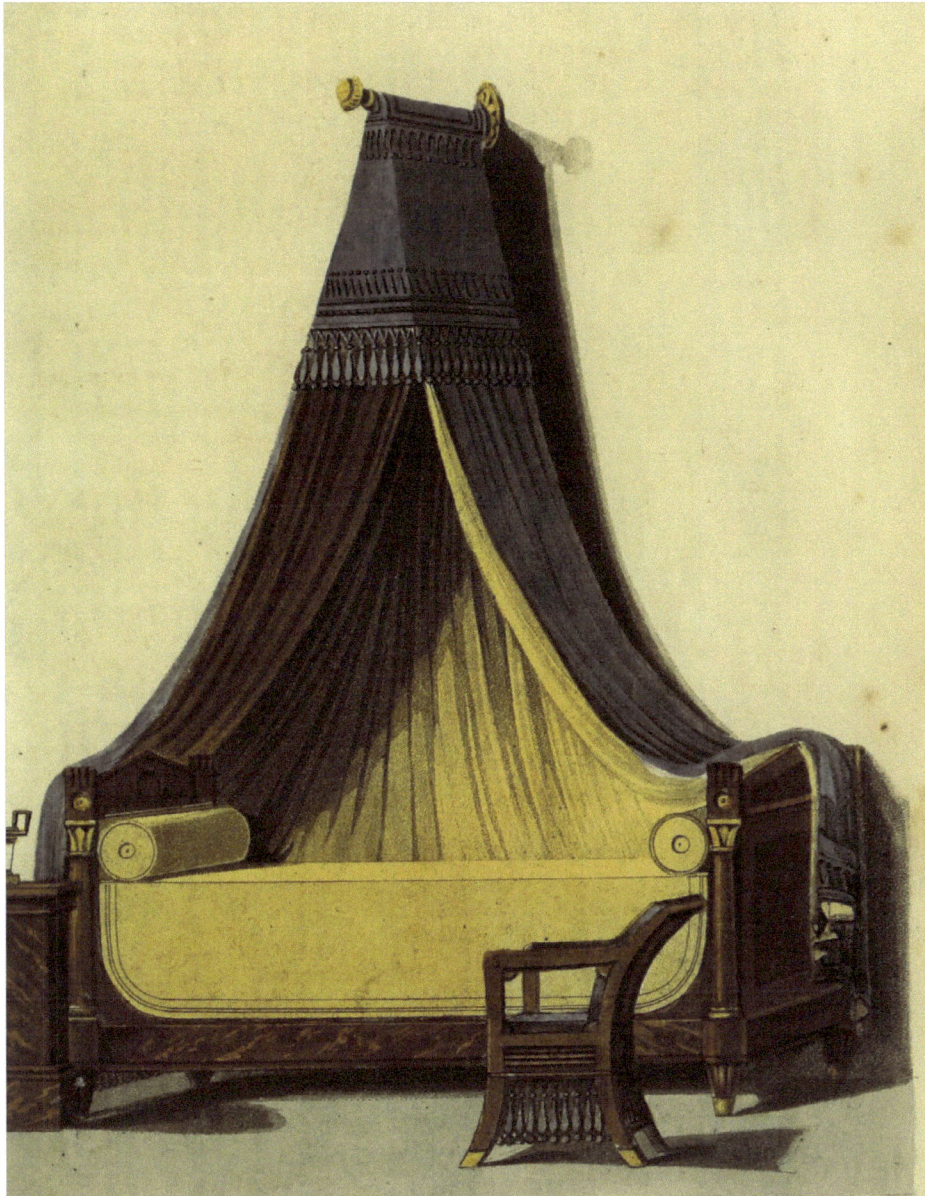

French Cottage Bed
February 1815

FRENCH COTTAGE BED

    The interchange of feeling between this country and France, as it relates to matters of taste, has not been wholly suspended during long and awful conflicts which have so greatly abridged the intercourse of the two nations, and as usual the taste of both has been improved; we have benefited by the fine fancy of the French artists, as they have not neglected to foster the results of British judgment in our own productions.

    From the peculiarities of our taste, the French have long adopted the cottage ornée and the English garden; but in the furniture of both, they have preserved much of their own style; for custom and habit do not readily submit even to the allurements of fashion. The furniture plate of the present month, represents a French cottage bed, as found in one of their country retreats: the drapery forms a tent-like canopy, and is suspended by a fasces projecting front the side of the room; the furniture is of a lilac silk, with deep yellow linings; the bed-frame is painted in imitation of rose-wood; the chair is of the same finishing, and the linings of it correspond with the bed-draperies.

Drawing-Room Window-Curtain
March 1815

DRAWING-ROOM WINDOW-CURTAIN

The manufacture of silks on which devices are interwoven in gradation of tints, and in the way which is termed shot, in harmony with the colour of the ground, afford a tasteful material for the furniture of the drawing-room and the boudoir. It is introduced in the plate for this month, which is intended to exhibit the furniture of a window, possessing the various parts to which the fashion of the day has given sanction, and forming a whole of peculiarly chaste and elegant character. The drapery is of azure blue, edged with the bullion fringe, or one of those excellent imitations of it which so readily deceive the eye even of the connoisseur. The metal pins are omitted, and the curtains are festooned by silken cords, embellished by tassels, which pass behind the cornice hangings: the rod and its ornaments are of metal, and the ground on which it stands is of matt gilding.

French Sofa
April 1815

FRENCH SOFA

The character of simplicity which belongs to this piece of furniture, and the materials of which it is composed, render it suitable for the library or morning-room. The outline of the seat and back are described by equal radii, and are intersected by small circles, that combine with them and form a long elipse or oval: the width of the seat, however, separating the line of the back; from the front, an intricacy is produced, which gives the sofa a peculiarly agreeable effect, and by this arrangement the back almost seems to be reflected in water: and indeed in furniture, a certain degree of uniformity is necessary to its composition, both on account of its being to assimilate with architecture, which is severe in this particular, and because a portion of this severity is essential to the character of beauty, dignity, and greatness. The frame may be composed of any of the variegated woods, and the seat and back of morocco, it being so in the original. A candelabrum, or reading-lamp, and a receptacle for flowers, form a portion of this plate.

Artisans Furniture
July 1815

ARTISANS FURNITURE

Our engraving this month exihibits a table, chair, and rack, adapted to the apartment of an artist or amateur; the whole are of mahogany. The table is provided with a desk capable of being raised or lowered at pleasure, and two drawers at each end for the purpose of holding the drawing materials, while a shelf beneath is destined to receive those books which are wanted for immediate reference. The chair, with stuffed seat, is lined with blue morocco, bordered with silk fringe and tassels of the same colour. The tops of the rack, supporting the portfolio of drawings, are also covered with blue morocco, bordered in the same manner as the chair. The chaste simplicity evinced as well in the general design as in the detail of these articles, which are nevertheless not destitute of a due degree of elegance, will not fail to strike every observer of taste, and recommend them to the imitation of those classes of persons for whose use they are intended.

Furniture for a Music Room
August 1815

FURNITURE FOR A MUSIC ROOM

The music-room has not failed to experience the patronage of our fair country-women, who, in the choice of its furniture, have selected forms appropriate to its uses, and established in its embellishments a character of beauty, which, at the same time that it harmonizes with the drawing-room, affords a most desirable variety with that more sumptuously decorated apartment. To pursue this object, the plate of the present month exhibits designs for an ordonnateur, a seat, a footstool, and a music-stand; in which a correspondence of style is preserved, on principles of graceful and simple elegance.

Boudoir Window-Curtains
September 1815

BOUDOIR WINDOW-CURTAINS

The annexed plate represents curtains designed for the boudoir or the breakfast-parlour, in a style of singular elegance and of moderate expence. The draperies are festooned, and suspended on consoles of Grecian forms, in black and burnished gold, the base being of a dark tea-green, ornamented with black velvet wreaths. The curtains are of fawn colour, with tea-green independent margins, to match the ground of tile consoles, and edged with black fringe: the windows are, in effect, united by the seeming connection of the vanneur, making a whole of great simplicity and richness. The muslin curtains are edged with a tea-green chenille: other colours may be adopted of course, but they should be arranged on similar principles, or there will be danger that the effect will fail to prove sufficiently chaste and corresponding with the prevailing fashion of the day.

Dinner-Room and Drawing-Room Chairs
October 1815

DINNER-ROOM AND DRAWING-ROOM CHAIRS

The design which forms the furniture plate of the present month, exhibits chairs that would be found very elegant in execution. No. I. for the dinner-room, is of mahogany, enriched by a small portion of carving and by inlaid devices of ebony; the seat is of morocco leather. No. 2. is a design of a very splendid character, and suited to the most embellished drawing-room; it may be formed of the lighter rose or other woods, and ornamented with gilt and silver devices, so arranged as to produce a rich and pleasing effect: a light blue cushion of silk, with tassels of gold or silver, is proper for this design. No. 3. is a chair for a drawing -room also; it may be formed of the darker rose or Coromandel wood, the ornaments being of or-molu, and the cushion plain silk, or of chintz drapery.

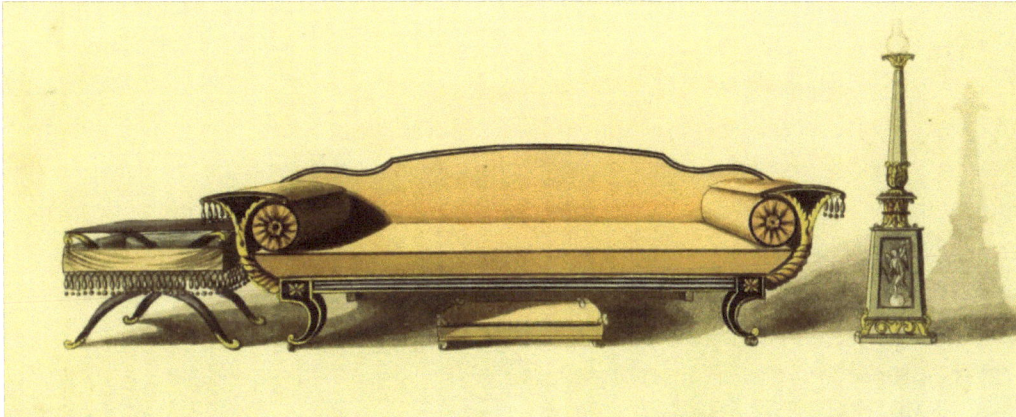

Sofa, Work-Table, and Candelabrum
November 1815

SOFA, WOKK-TABLE, AND CANDELABRUM

The repository of Messrs. Morgan and Saunders has supplied the materials for the annexed plate. The sofa is novel and elegant, and affords a peculiar means of ease and repose, by the tabular cushions that are formed at each end, which unite with the round ones, and seem to embody them in the sofa itself. This sofa is the best adapted for the enjoyment of reading and study of all we have yet seen, and the design is correctly ornamental. The book and work-table correspond with the sofa; and the candelabrum is suitable to the support of an argand lamp, or the globe for a gas-light. The principles on which the sofa and the work-table are designed, would combine admirably with the Chinese style, and form very elegant pieces of furniture for rooms so decorated.

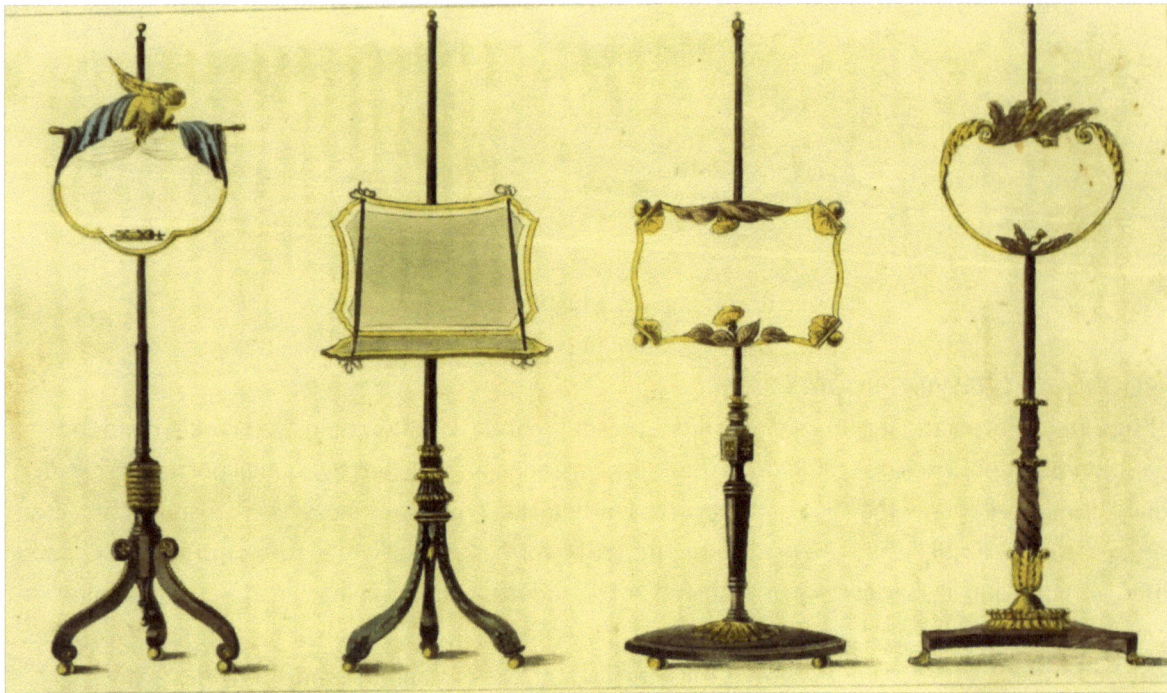

Fire Screens
December 1815

FIRE SCREENS

The talent for drawing, which has been cultivated with so much success by some ladies of high rank, enabled them to decorate several articles of furniture in a very novel and tasteful manner. A laudable emulation in the higher circles caused this species of art to become a fashion, and an extensive variety of ornamental furniture has been produced by ladies; many articles of which have lost nothing even in comparison with the works of very clever professional artists.

There are few pieces of furniture so appropriate to the purpose of decoration in this style as the screen either for the hand, or to be supported by poles; four designs for the latter are introduced in the annexed plate; they exhibit the proportions and forms applicable, which may be ornamented as the taste of the amateur may suggest, either by figures, landscapes, vases, flowers, or simply by Etruscan or embossed gold borders. Small paravents would afford ample means for the exercise of the elegant talent of design, and be beautiful and useful appendages to the drawing-room.

A Chimney-Piece of Mona Marble
January 1816

A CHIMNEY-PIECE OF MONA MARBLE

The subject of the annexed plate is a chimney-piece and stove, the former being executed of the Mona marble, and ornamented with bronze or or-molu; the design is from Mr. Bullock's extensive and tasteful repository in Tenterden- street, Hanover-square. The importance of this invaluable marble to the purposes of interior decoration, renders the discovery of it highly interesting, as it vies in richness of colour with the precious marbles of antiquity, and affords to the artist, at a reasonable price, a means for this splendid decoration, and for combining it with the colours of the apartment and the furniture. — The columns of the Repository will not afford space to notice adequately the merits both of the material and tasteful feeling with which the articles of Mr. Bullock's manufactory are composed; but an early opportunity will be taken to describe the excellencies of the Mona marble, and of his peculiar applications of it and of the British oak to splendid furniture.

Drawing-Room Window-Curtain and Cabinet
February 1816

DRAWING-ROOM WINDOW-CURTAIN AND CABINET

The annexed plate represents the window side of a small drawing-room, embellished with curtains disposed in a very tasteful manner; the two windows are embraced, and a feature of greatness elegantly produced by the upper draperies; which afford also a beautiful combination of lines and colour, further enriched by cords, tassels, and the gilding of the central rosette, and the Thyrsis' ends.

The cabinet is designed for execution in our native woods, relieved by inlaid metal ornaments; a style happily introduced, both in respect of taste and true patriotism. There are no woods more beautiful, or better suited to the purposes of cabinet embellishment, than those indigenous in our own country.

We are obliged to Mr. C. Bullock for permission to present our readers with this specimen of his manufactory.

Lit De Repoś
March 1815

LIT DE REPOŚ

In fashions, as in manners, it sometimes happens, that one extreme immediately usurps the place of the other, without regarding their intervening degrees of approximation. For the precise, in dress, the French have adopted the deshabille; and it has been applied to their articles of furniture in many instances, giving to them an air which the amateurs term the négligé.

In the annexed plate the design of a lit de repoś, or sofa-bed, has a peculiar character of unaffected ease, and is not without its full claims to elegance. The sofa is of the usual construction, and the draperies are thrown over a sceptre-rod projecting from the wall of the apartment: they are of silk, as is the courte-pointe also.

A French Bed
April 1816

A FRENCH BED

The annexed plate is a design lately imported from Paris, and represents one of those pieces of furniture which are consequent on the reciprocal exchanges of British and French taste: it is an English bed with corner posts, decorated agreeably to Parisian fancy. The frame-work is made of rose-wood, ornamented with carved foliage, gilt in matt and burnished gold.

The drapery is of rose-coloured silk, lined with azure blue, and consists of one curtain, gathered up at the ring in the centre of the canopy, being full enough to form the festoons and curtains both of the head and foot. The elegance of this bed greatly depends on the choice, arrangement, and modifications of the three primitive colours, blue, yellow, and red; and in the combination of these, its chasteness or gaiety may be augmented or abridged.

Grecian Furniture
May 1816

GRECIAN FURNITURE

So long as it is the fashion to render the apartments of our habitations dependent for their embellishment on a display of elegant furniture and draperies, rather than on those features which are peculiarly and legitimately architectural!, the public must be congratulated, that men of genius and science are found to devote their attention to that particular branch of art. Art indeed it may properly be called, when the designs of this species of embellishment embrace the combinations of form, composition, light, shade, and colour, and are as classically united agreeably to the laws of fitness and truth, as they are found to be in the works of masters eminent in the walks of pictorial beauty. It is impossible to examine the furniture of Mr. G. Bullock's manufactory in Tenterden-street, of which the plate represents a part, without feeling the propriety of this congratulation; and the liberality with which he permits us to give his designs to the public, obliges us to acknowledge it.

This representation of Grecian furniture is intended to form part of the decoration of a library: attached to the sofa, are cabinets for the purpose of receiving portfolios or splendid manuscripts, and form elegant pedestals, which are surmounted by fine specimens of the

Mona verd - antique marble, on which may be placed urns for flowers or perfume. These cabinets are enriched by or-molu, forming unique and most convenient pieces of furniture. The plate itself forms an elegant picture, and the group consists of a sofa, monopodium, footstool, pictures, and drapery, affording a specimen of harmonious decoraton and colouring.

84

Dining-Room Window-Curtain and Sideboard
June 1816

DINING-ROOM CURTAIN AND SIDEBOARD

The annexed plate represents a portion of a dining-room, containing designs of a sideboard, and other appendages to this apartment. A recess, circular at each end, is formed to receive the side-board; which does not, therefore, curtail the length of the room, and so proportions the pannel as to receive a glass of moderate dimensions, over which is an appropriate tablet of figures. A cellaret is beneath, and candelabrum on each side. The curtain is of a very simple construction, being passed over the pole, from which it falls and terminates in a figured and fringed border.

A Saloon
July 1816

A SALOON

The designs of many of our villas, particularly those erected about forty or fifty years ago, contained circular-topped windows to the central, and in some cases to all the apartments of the ground floor; and although it has been usual in such cases to consider the windows as square-topped, concealing the spandrels by the upper draperies, yet the opportunity of producing a variety of form in the designs of furniture is very desirable. The annexed plate therefore represents draperies suited to such windows; the arrangement of which, from its architectural and simple elegance.

The saloon being an apartment of communication, and through which the principal rooms are approached, the prevailing colours should harmonize with them and yet be of such cool or subdued character as will produce in the others an effect of greater brilliancy. The curtains may, notwithstanding, have that character of richness that will give importance to the saloon, and allow it to join with the superior apartments in effecting a general richness and splendour.

Dining-Room Window-Curtains
August 1816

DINING-ROOM WINDOW-CURTAINS

Perhaps no furniture is more decorative and graceful than that of which draperies form a considerable part: the easy disposition of the folds of curtains and other hangings, the sweep of the lines composing their forms, and the harmonious combinations of their colours, produced a charm that brought them into high repute, but eventually occasioned their use in so liberal a degree, as in many instances to have clothed up the ornamented walls, and in others they have been substituted entirely for their more genuine decorations, by which the rooms obtained the air of a mercer's or draper's shop in full display of its merchandize, rather than the well-imagined and correctly designed apartment of a British edifice: indeed, to so great an excess was the system of ornamental finishing by draperies carried, that it became the usual observation of a celebrated amateur in this way, that he would be quite satisfied if a well-proportioned barn was provided, and he would in a week convert it, by such means, into a drawing-room of the first style and fashion. So long as novelty favoured the application, this redundance was tolerated; but time has brought the uses of these draperies to their proper office of conforming to the original design, consisting of those architectural combinations that possess a far greater beauty, dignity, and variety, than draperies are capable of affording.

The annexed plate represents part of a dining-room, in which curtains are so introduced, that the forms of the piers, imposts, and architraves, are not concealed by their projections, but in which they most elegantly occupy the station and quantity of space that properly belong to them. This furniture has been executed by Mr. G. Bullock.

A Small Bed
September 1816

A SMALL BED

The annexed design represents a bed intended for the apartment of a young lady of fashion. The hangings are of light blue silk, the ornaments being a tender shade of brown, and the linings to correspond; they are supported by rings and rods of brass, behind which the curtains are suspended, and drawn up by silk cords, enriched with tassels. This design has been so executed, and had a very elegant and rich effect: it would, however, be suitable to draperies of the usual material.

In the present state of our silk-manufactories, the adoption of a similar style of furniture for our apartments would prove a national advantage.

Mona Marble Chimney-Piece
October 1816

MONA MARBLE CHIMNEY-PIECE

The Mona marble has so considerably increased in reputation and fashion that no apology needs be offered for presenting our readers with the annexed design, which shews the simple forms proper to receive the ornaments of bronze, or or-molu, with which these chimney-pieces are usually ornamented for apartments of superior decoration. From the circumstance of this simplicity of design, they are manufactured at prices calculated to supersede similar works in foreign white marbles, over which they have a considerable advantage, from the beautifully variegated tints of the Mona marble, and from the circumstance of its preserving the original freshness of effect, which statuary loses in a few years.

An English Bed
November 1816

AN ENGLISH BED

    The drawing for this plate was taken by permission of Mr. G. Bullock, in whose manufactory the design was executed, and it was selected for the tasteful simplicity that pervades it. The abandonment of that profusion of drapery which has long been fashionable, has admitted this more chastened style in point of forms, and introduced a richness in point of colours that has long been neglected. This splendid character, if followed with discretion, will speedily supersede the present cold and cheerless effect of our apartments, which have little pretension to the term embellished until the furniture is placed within them.

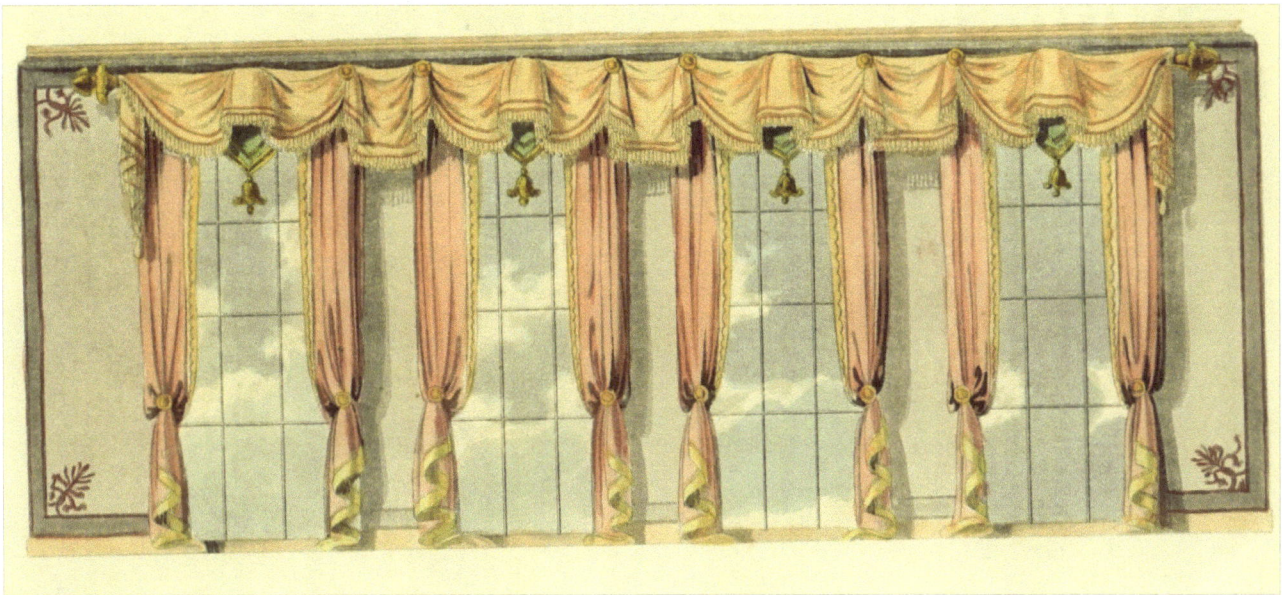

Drawing-Room Window-Curtain
December 1816

DRAWING-ROOM WINDOW-CURTAIN

The window side of a drawing- room, furnished with draperies of peculiar elegance, is represented by the annexed plate, the design of which is from the manufactory Mr. Bullock Tenterden-street. There is a richness united with simplicity in the forms of this arrangement, that is very pleasing, and the colours are happily disposed to exhibit them to advantage.

Drawing-Room Window-Curtain
April 1817

DRAWING-ROOM WINDOW-CURTAIN

The window side of a small draw-room is represented in this engraving, as it has been executed by Mr. G. Bullock, of Tenterden-street. The arrangement of the colours, and their respective quantities, are agreeable to the practice of our best artists in their pictorial works. The draperies are elegantly disposed, and the whole forms an embellishment suited to apartments in the most fashionable style of decoration.

Gothic Chimneypiece in Mona Marble
June 1817

GOTHIC CHIMNEYPIECE IN MONA MARBLE

This design is suitable to the dining-parlour of a mansion in the Gothic style of architecture, the parts being selected from the best works of the fourteenth and fifteenth centuries. The fire-grate is also composed to assimilate with the general character or such a building; with which, indeed, every part of the furniture should accord, as few things are so disgusting to the eye of taste as t lie incongruous mixture which is often seen, even in expensively furnished houses, where the Grecian and Gothic, the Roman and the Chinese styles are absurdly jumbled together. As the Gothic forms admit of a very splendid decoration in point of colour, the Mona marble for that purpose is a useful material in the hands of a tasteful architect.

Fashionable Chairs
September 1817

FASHIONABLE CHAIRS

The annexed plate represents chairs from the repository of Mr. G. Bullock, and they are designed for apartments of three different modes of building: the centre chair is intended for a Grecian library, that to the right of it for a suite of rooms in the Gothic style, and that on the left for a book-room in a mansion built in the seventeenth century. Although the forms are good, and well adapted to the purpose for which they are designed, yet the materials with which they are composed, and the excellence of their workmanship, give an importance and value to them, that is not to be exhibited by a graphical representation.

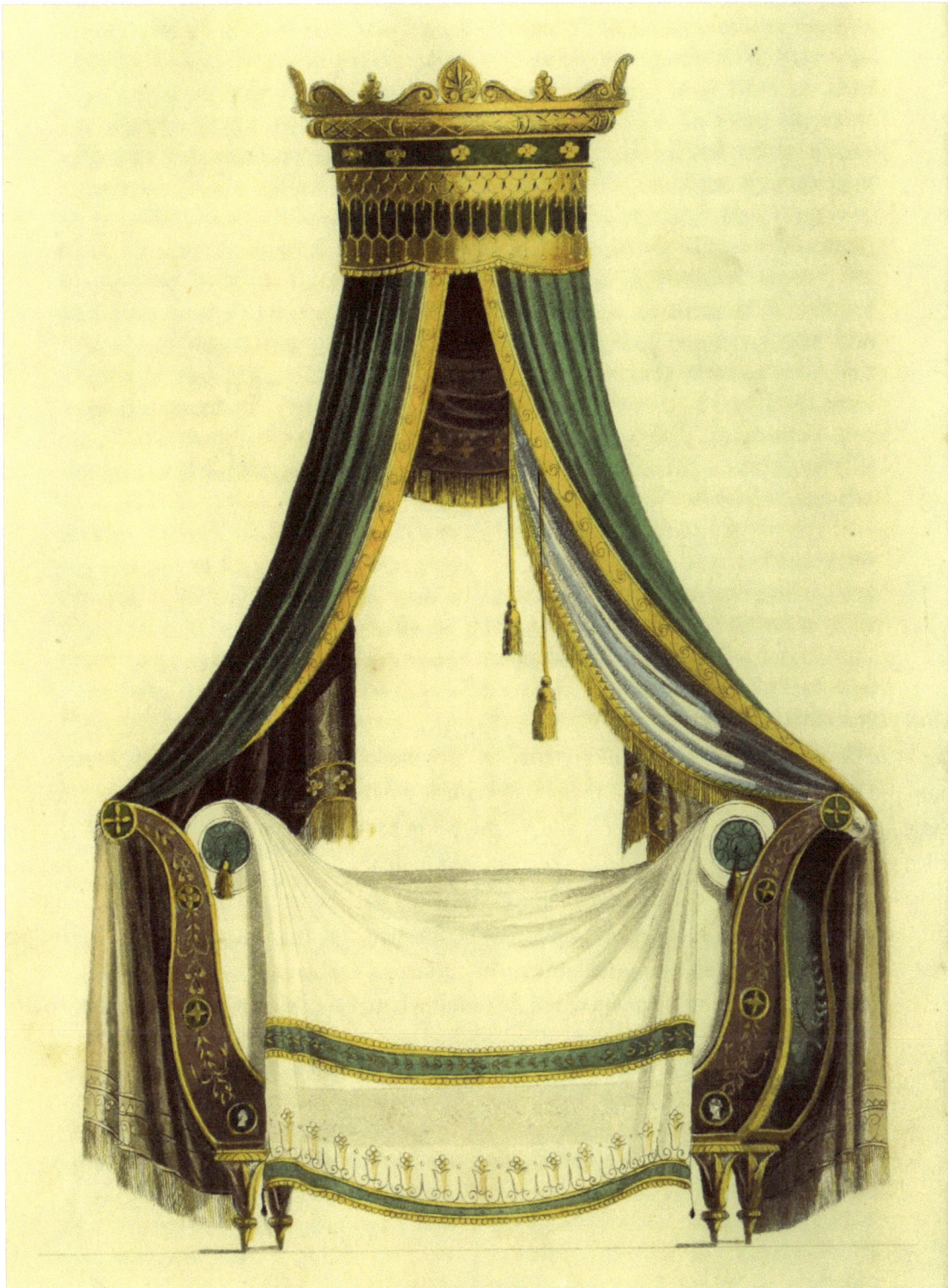

A French Bed
October 1817

A FRENCH BED

   The annexed plate represents a superb canopy and sofa-bed: the draperies are of silk, and ornamented with the lace and fringe which are so admirable an imitation of gold; the linings are of lilac and buff. A muslin embroidered drapery is applied as a covering in the daytime. There is an elegant simplicity united with so much richness in this design, that our readers will perceive it is adapted to chambers in the first style of decoration.

An Ottoman for a Gallery
November 1817

AN OTTOMAN FOR A GALLERY

This species of furniture has been introduced to us, as its name implies, from one of those Eastern nations where the habits of the people make them necessary — a people whose love of ease has taught them to devise ample means for its indulgence; and for this purpose the Ottoman is well calculated.

The design represented by the annexed plate corresponds in general form to the furniture alluded to, but its embellishments make it suitable to apartments in the usual style of decoration. The framework is composed of the valuable woods enriched with carved work, finished in burnished gold. The draperies are buff-coloured velvet, the pattern being embroidered on its surface, and bounded by bullion lace.

Should it be required to have the Ottoman of greater length, it may be extended without injury to the design.

A Pier Table and Grecian Pedestal
August 1818

A PIER TABLE AND GRECIAN PEDESTAL

This design forms a sumptuous piece of furniture, that is adapted to the apartment of an officer of high rank, or to embellish one of those establishments devoted to military gentlemen. The table is supposed to bear a large pier glass, the frame of which is finished in gold, and velvet of a colour corresponding with the draperies, and ornamented by devices carved and gilt. The shelf, or table-top, is of verd-antique marble, supported by gold fasces. The plinth and margins are of rose-wood, or of the oak transversely cut and highly polished, which in splendour rivals the foreign woods, and admirably harmonizes with surrounding decorations. These are ornamented by the sword and spear, and by laurel- branches above them. The panels are of two designs, forming circular compartments, the margins of which are velvet, white, and gold.

The panel on the left of the design is embellished by the mask of Apollo, and radii in gold, forming the well known symbol of the power of that deity.

The pedestal is designed to correspond in style and materials, and is suited to bear a group of figures in bronze or or-molu, terminated by branches for lights. These are properly placed in the angles of large rooms, that will otherwise be gloomy in those parts, however the apartment may he generally well lighted.

Design for a Commode, Pier Glass, and Tabourets
November 1818

DESIGN FOR A COMMODE, PIER GLASS, AND TABOURETS

This furniture was intended for a saloon of an octagonal form, four sides of which were occupied by entrances to several apartments, and the four remaining sides by glasses and commodes: as each reflected an opposite pier, they produced effects called the endless perspective, so much admired in the present arrangement of this species of furniture; and repeating the magnificent lustre suspended from the centre of the ceiling of the apartment, the brilliant vistas formed by their seeming continuity were particularly striking.

This commode is proposed to be formed of the American maple-wood, with a statuary-marble top, and the ornaments in gold: the panels are of verd antique, to give effect to the basso-relievo of ivory; a style of embellishment superseding the bronze, and in high estimation if well executed.

The glass-frame is a pale lavender, and the ornaments are in gold. The tabourets are of maple-wood and gold, and the draperies of rich purple.

The apartment in which a similar arrangement should be adopted, must be previously designed in a corresponding style of Grecian symmetry, or the effect and beauty would be would be imperfect.

95

Drawing-Room Window-Curtain
December 1818

DRAWING-ROOM WINDOW-CURTAIN

The draperies of this design are arranged and decorated in the style of the Vatican embellishments, and are suspended from a cornice by silk cords and tassels; the curtains are edged by a border of foliages and figures in lozenges, ovals, and other formed tablets. The material with which they are composed is an exquisitely fine woollen cloth, on which the border is painted by hand, as is frequently done on velvet; and the cornice is decorated in a similar way, with the addition of gold fillets and moulding. The sub-curtain is of muslin, withdrawn by cords and tassels.

Drawing-Room Window-Curtain and Jardinière
March 1819

DRAWING-ROOM WINDOW-CURTAIN AND JARDINIERE

This suite of draperies is adapted to a bow-window with considerable taste and elegance; they are fancifully suspended from carved devices, relating to vintage and the splendour of the year; indicative of which, the central ornament is a golden peacock, whose displayed plumage being delicately coloured in parts, so as to imitate the richness of its nature, the effect is considerably increased.

The swags are arranged with an easy lightness, and the festoons with unusual variety of size and form; they are composed of light blue silk, and lined with pink taffeta.

The jardinière forms a proper ornament for such a situation, and is rendered particularly interesting by a font of gold and silver fish, and by a small aviary for choice singing birds: the style is French, and the article similar in design to those executed at Paris under the direction of Mons. Percier, the architect.

We are indebted for the materials of the annexed plate to the liberality of Mr. John Stafford, an eminent upholsterer at Bath.

Gothic Furniture
April 1819

GOTHIC FURNITURE

The annexed examples are of that unsystemised art which is often called Gothic, hut which should properly be termed *Tedeschi*, or *old German*, being of the style which was substituted for the Greek and Roman forms of the purer ages. The Italians, to designate this perversion of art, called every departure from the genuine models by the name of Gothic, although widely differing from the style adopted by the Saxons and the Goths; and left it to later times to give name to each particular style that the feeling and genius of any people might cultivate.

The style of furniture exhibited, prevailed in the mansions of the first rank in Germany in the fifteenth century; and although a purer taste has succeeded, from the high cultivation of art in that country, yet its fitness and correspondence to some of our own ancient buildings render the annexed examples of genuine Tedeschi furniture very desirable.

Dining-Room Suite
May 1819

A DESIGN FOR A DINING-ROOM SUITE, CURTAINS EXCEPTED, IN ORDER TO SHEW MORE PARTICULARLY THE LINES OF THE WINDOW-ARCHITRAVE AND FRENCH CASEMENT

The casement of the cornice may be of mat gold, or covered with black velvet; in the centre and ends of which are pine-apples, with their natural leafing: clusters of grapes and leaves, carved, are formed on a strong wire (previously interwoven), to entwine the cornice. The piers may be embellished with busts of our most illustrious military and naval commanders, sustained by pedestals decorated with appropriate trophies, or designs, commemorative of their individual achievements.

Drawing-Room Window-Curtain and Work-Table
August 1819

DRAWING-ROOM WINDOW-CURTAIN

This design is supplied by Mr. Stafford, upholsterer, of Bath, and represents an elegant drapery of light green silk and pink taffeta linings; the sub-curtains are of clear muslin.

The festoon draperies are supported by the eagle of Jupiter embracing the thunderbolt, by arrows which have pierced the wall, and by termini of foliages: these draperies are decorated by an embossed applique border, which forms double rows upon the festoons, and divides the curtains from the extreme supports, over which it falls, as if suspended by them; the curtains are also bordered by a silk open fringe.

The work-table is designed to be richly carved and gilt; and is a tripod supporting a circular tablet, which contains the necessary articles for the species of employment to which it is dedicated. When the pier between the windows is narrow, and the proportion of the windows themselves admits of being thus formed into the character of a single window, these draperies would be highly ornamental.

Drawing-Room Window-Curtains
September 1819

DRAWING-ROOM WINDOW-CURTAINS

The designs for these draperies were supplied by Mr. Stafford, upholsterer, of Bath: they consist of two complete decorations, dissimilar only in point of arrangement, the materials and colours being the some in both. The curtains are supported by fasces carved and gilt, and ornamented by antique scroll foliages. The draperies on: the right of the plate are adapted to a boudoir or morning-room, and those on the left to a drawing-room; and it will be found, in practice, that the latter would have a very tasteful and elegant effect, particularly if the number of windows should permit a greater display of them in connection or succession.

The very narrow space between the windows of this design is not suitable to a pier glass, and when such abridged divisions occur, they cannot be better furnished than according to the proposed intention. In the first, a candelabrum supporting a clock is introduced; and the latter is ornamented by a marble, bronze, or or-molu figure.

Library Window-Curtain
October 1819

LIBRARY WINDOW-CURTAIN

A plain drapery for a library or study, executed by Mr. Stafford of Bath, of moreen or velvet, which is formed into large pipes filled with wool, and is sewn to a piece of coarse canvas, which is previously prepared to the lengths, depth and shape of the facia. The pipes may he ornamented with plain or appliqued velvet, as is shewn on the curtains. A small gilded bead of wood is to be appended at the lower edge and finish of the pipes, under which a very full net-work fringe is fixed with card-tacks. The depth of the facia and the fringe must of course be guided by the extent of dead-light. The tablet in the centre is covered plain, and embellished with a figure of Meditation; the back-ground is composed of minor objects, emblematical of the subject; and the whole is carved in alto-relievo. A terminus in the pier supports a globe on the platform, the interior being a depository for manuscripts; it also contains a clock-movement, the dial of which presents itself on the outside, surmounted with an appropriate device of Mercury.

Three Designs for Window-Curtains
December 1819

THREE DESIGNS FOR WINDOW-CURTAINS

An ingenious artist will communicate to the commonest theme an inexhaustible variety of design: in doing this he must, however, give *liberty* to his ideas, which, if well instructed in the first instance, will never take their flight beyond the limits prescribed by fitness and true taste. The imagination so controuled is properly distinguished from *fancy*, which wantonly oversteps all limitations, and trespasses alike on the most sacred and on the profanest grounds of *theory* and *practice*; and hence the distinction between the works of an artist and of an amateur, as well in the higher departments of art, as in that of mere upholstery.

The annexed subject presents features of perfect novelty, without a departure from its guiding principles. The centre draperies, in two colours, are composed for a Venetian or Palladian window: they are supported by a bow-like ornament, and by pilasters, to which the curtains are connected the sub-curtains are also festooned by the bow, and guarded by a lateral transom, that passes from pilaster to pilaster.

The designs on the right and left are light and elegant: they should be composed of silk, and the sub-curtains of transparent materials richly embroidered: so executed, the delicacy of their combinations makes them suitable to a cabinet or boudoir.

For these designs we are indebted to Mr. Stafford of Bath.

Draperies for Circular Windows
February 1820

DRAPERIES FOR CIRCULAR WINDOWS

The annexed plate represents a bow, forming a recess of bay in the tasteful drawing-room, and in which three windows are supposed to e erected: they are furnished by a suite of draperies, supported by a compass-rod and appliqué carved ornaments: the forms are varied, easy and elegant; the colours chaste, and well arranged for effect and harmony. This embellishment is highly creditable to Mr. Stafford of Bath, from whose upholstery depot it proceeds; for he has her ably surmounted many difficulties that are common to bow windows, and to those situated as represented in the present design.

Draperies for Drawing-Room Windows
March 1820

DRAPERIES FOR DRAWING-ROOM WINDOWS

Apartments the best suited to this decoration are those that have in them ranges of windows in uneven numbers, as three, five, seven, or nine; but in that of three more particularly, such draperies are usually disposed with the best effect; and in the annexed design, Mr. Stafford, upholsterer, of Bath, has taken advantage of the agreeable disposition of the windows there represented, to display a graceful contour of continued festoons, calculated to embrace a further number of windows, and to a considerable extent.

The playful external swags in are blue are properly relieved by the buff sub-curtains, which are more simply arranged in Greek mantle forms, and are made to combine with the white transparent veils in the well-approved harmony of colour constituted by blue and buff.

Draperies for Drawing-Room Windows
May 1820

DRAPERIES FOR DRAWING-ROOM WINDOWS

A paladian window of three divisions is here proposed to be decorated by curtains of blue and lilac silk and taffeta: as these colours have affinity to each other, the lilac being a mixture of blue and red, they need contrast and harmonizing by some other colour: thus, for this purpose gilt carved supports, gold-coloured lines, tassels, fringes, and trimmings, are liberally introduced, being alike harmonious with the lilac and the blue.

The white transparent curtains are suspended in plain masses, for the purpose of general relief, rendering the whole brilliantly effective, by such means as painters employ when they introduce the three primitive colours and white in combination, to obtain a high degree of splendour by simple arrangements.

Window-Draperies
June 1820

WINDOW-DRAPERIES

The three designs for window-draperies in the annexed plate, are suited to small apartments. The first is composed of a single festoon, supported by a rich ornamented and gilt bow, in a simple yet elegant manner. The last design is more varied, and consists of a double festoon, with rich cornice. The middle design presents only draperies on a carved pole: here the festoon is formed by the junction of half-swags, and has a novel effect. The colours introduced are light blue and delicate fawn, relieved by white muslin sub-curtains, of large pattern.

It will be perceived, that, by a little contrivance, these curtains will assist in the formation of other designs, by an interchange of their positions; and for this purpose they are presented together.

Draperies for a Half-Sexagon Bow Window
July 1820

DRAPERIES TOR A HALF-SEXAGON BOW WINDOW

A jardinière is here introduced as an elegant article suited to a drawing-room, and which likewise serves to furnish the vacancy otherwise occasioned by the shape of the window. The upper figure, as well as the group below, may be sculptured in marble, or carved in wood; and the basket which springs from the cistern, may be composed of wicker-work, painted green, or any other soft and subservient colour. The cistern, being lined with tin or fine sheet lead, might be made to contain a great assemblage of foliage, and a proper provision of water would render it at all times buoyant. Pot-pourri jars may be introduced in the receptacle below, encircled with brass treillage.

It is to the taste of Mr. Stafford of Bath, that we are indebted for this design.

Window-Drapery
September 1820

WINDOW-DRAPERY

Curtain-cornices are now adopted in great variety, and will probably very soon supersede the late fashion of suspending draperies by poles and detached ornaments. The annexed design represents draperies to three windows, surmounted by a fanciful continued cornice, embracing them all; this is a little elevated, and arched in the centre, to form a canopy and throne-like character, and commence a vista, where a statue is placed to increase the effect.

The carved work of the cornice is gilt, and a gold-edged valance, formed of Merino cloth and velvet, completes its lower surface. The curtains are of pink silk or figured chintz, finished by an embossed scroll border, and the sub- draperies are of white muslin.

JODY GAYLE, bestselling author and researcher, likens her work to that of a literary archeologist rather than a traditional author or imperator of history. She is dedicated to unearthing publications of the past, and sharing these long-forgotten books... the jewels and riches of the written word. She has uncovered tens of thousands of old publications from the eighteenth and nineteenth centuries and wants to bring them to life, and send her readers traveling back in time.

About Jody...

* She grew up on a farm in a small town of about 500 people and first learned to drive on a tractor. She can milk a cow as easily as pluck a chicken.

* Stood within twenty feet of the first node of the International Space Station. Unfortunately, her feet were firmly planted on the earth at the time.

* Has gone whitewater rafting and horseback riding in the mountains of Montana. She has swum with dolphins and sharks, and refueled a fighter jet in the sky on an Air Force KC135. Jody is a bit of an adventurer.

* Jody and her son share the same birthday -- New Year's Day!

She loves to hear from her readers. Visit her website and Facebook page.

Thank you for reading
FASHIONS IN THE ERA OF JANE AUSTEN

If you enjoyed this book, I would appreciate it if you'd help other readers enjoy it, too. After all, most books are purchased due to word-of-mouth recommendations. How can you help?

Recommend it. Please help other readers find this book by recommending it to friends, readers' groups, and discussion boards.

Review it. Please tell other readers why you liked this book by reviewing it on Amazon, Goodreads, or your blog. If you write a review, please send me a copy at jody@jodygayle.com